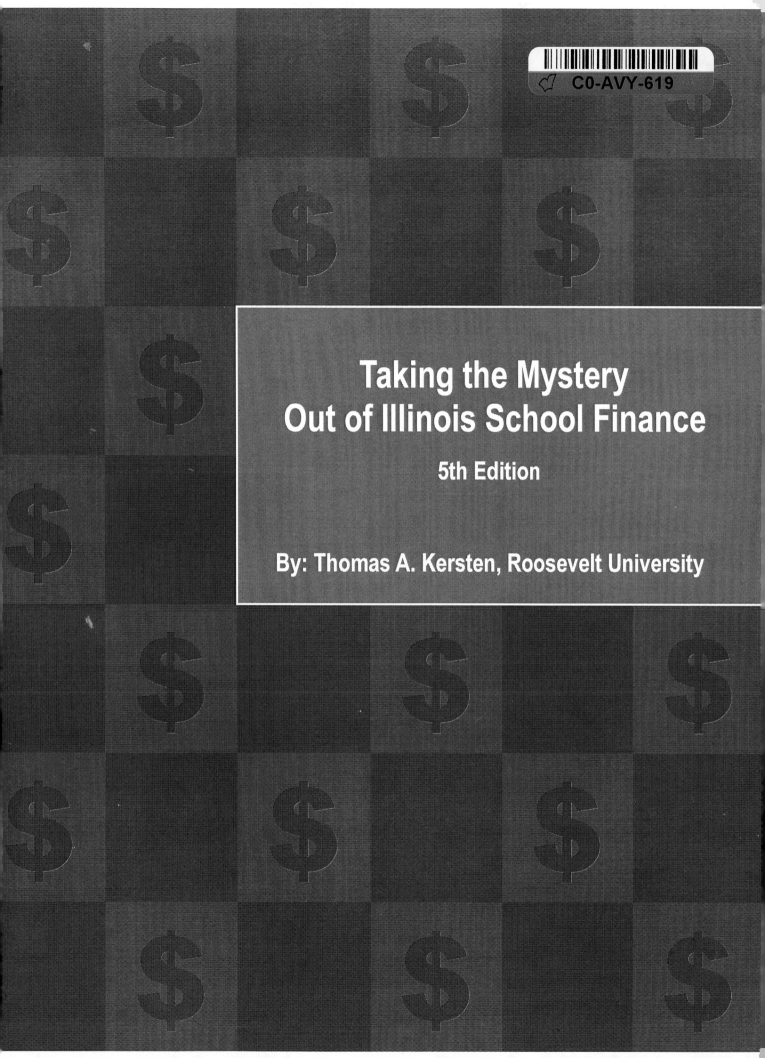

Taking the Mystery Out of Illinois School Finance

5th Edition

By: Thomas A. Kersten, Roosevelt University

fifth edition

Taking the Mystery Out of

Illinois School Finance

Thomas A. Kersten

NCPEA Publications

National Council of Professors of Educational Administration

Ypsilanti, Michigan

Published by NCPEA Publications
The publications of the National Council of Professors of Educational Administration (NCPEA)
http://www.ncpeapublications.org

Printed in United States of America

Library of Congress Cataloging-in-Publication Data

Kersten, Thomas A.
Taking the mystery out of Illinois school finance
ISBN 978-1-4675-0166-8 (pbk)

How to order this book:

NCPEA Press, a book publisher for NCPEA Publications offers *Taking the Mystery Out of Illinois School Finance* as a Print-on-Demand hard copy at: http://www.lulu.com/content/paperback-book/taking-the-mystery-out-of-illinois-school-finance/13014148 Books are prepared in Perfect Bound binding and delivery is 3-5 days.

Taking the Mystery Out of Illinois School Finance has been peer reviewed, accepted, and endorsed by the National Council of Professors of Educational Administration as a significant contribution to the preparation and practice of school administration.

NCPEA Publications Director, Theodore B. Creighton
NCPEA Publications Technical Editor, Brad E. Bizzell

Contents

Acknowledgments

I would like to acknowledge three important individuals whose assistance was critical in helping me take the complex topic of Illinois school finance and make it much more understandable for those with limited school finance knowledge and experience.

Most of all I want to thank my wife Beth, Assistant Superintendent for Business Services in Skokie School District 68, for not only her patience and support throughout the writing process but also the invaluable background knowledge and critical assistance she provided through countless hours of conversation, editing, and revision.

Also, I want to acknowledge my good friend and former superintendent colleague, Dr. Nelson Armour, whose ongoing review and support helped shape the focus and content of this book. In addition, I want to recognize Dr. Bill Phillips, Associate Professor, at the University of Illinois at Springfield, for his assistance with the chapter on borrowing.

Special thanks to the resources and support provided by Virginia Tech and Theodore Creighton, NCPEA Publications Director.

Taking the Mystery Out of Illinois School Finance, 5th Edition

Taking the Mystery Out of Illinois School Finance, which was first published in 2007, is annually revised to reflect the most up-to-date information on Illinois school finance available. As such, it provides school administrators, school board members, professors, graduate students, and other stakeholders with an easy to understand explanation of school funding. What makes this book so unique is that it is the only comprehensive Illinois school finance resource readily available today.

Taking the Mystery Out of Illinois School Finance, 5th Edition has been significantly updated this year. In addition to providing the latest facts, figures, and legal requirements, it has been expanded to include more topics especially related to revenues, financial projections, and emerging issues.

Chapter 1

Understanding the Basic School Finance Principle

INTRODUCTION

The very mention of school finance to teachers, many school administrators, school board members, and other public school stakeholders usually conjures up images of jargon laden school district presentations, complicated reports, or graduate school textbooks, which seem designed to make anyone except school business officials feel confused and inadequate. For most people, school finance appears to be a quagmire of complex terms, formulas, and difficult to understand state and federal laws that are somehow inexplicably linked to both state and local politics.

To appreciate this point, consider this. Just show someone a copy of your most recent property tax bill and ask them to explain the state equalizer or the difference between assessed and equalized assessed valuation. You are likely to receive a blank stare. If you really want to confuse someone, just point to the drop in their local school district tax rate on their tax bill from last year and ask them to explain how the school portion of their property taxes increased. Too often school finance is presented just this way even to graduate students in Master of Arts programs in educational leadership. Given this traditional approach, is it any wonder that most educators find school finance very confusing?

Several years ago, a school board member in the school district where I was superintendent suggested an ingenious test to judge how clearly we were communicating with our stakeholders. We ultimately named it the 7-Eleven Test. It was simultaneously a complex yet simple way to judge whether we were effective communicators. The premise behind the 7-Eleven Test is this. No matter what educational program or issue you have, you should be able to walk down to your local 7-Eleven and explain it in such a way that anyone in the store can understand you.

One of the communication problems we often have as school administrators, especially in the area of school district finances, is that we have not emphasized the 7-Eleven Test enough. In fact, most of the time when we discuss school finance, we do so in such excessive educational jargon and excruciating detail that even many school administrators cannot comprehend it.

This book, *Taking the Mystery Out of Illinois School Finance*, is written with the 7-Eleven Test in mind. It is designed to explain the key principles of Illinois school finance in a way that graduate students, teachers, school board members, parents, building-level school administrators, and other interested citizens can grasp the essential content without getting bogged down in excessive financial detail. Only by understanding the basics of Illinois school finance, can school administrators, board members, and other constituents make informed decisions.

THE CENTRAL THEME – REVENUES VERSUS EXPENDITURES

The general principle behind school finance is actually quite simple. In its most basic form, school finance is a two-sided equation with revenues on one side and expenditures on the other. If revenues meet or exceed expenses regularly, your school district is financially solvent. However, when expenses start to exceed revenues, particularly over multiple years, the school district is probably heading toward financial difficulty, sometimes even if it has a large cash reserve.

A good way to understand this basic principle is to relate school finances to personal finances. Let's assume that you earn $50,000 per year. If your expenses are below $50,000 annually and expected to remain so for the foreseeable future, you are financially solvent. That is, you have more income than you need. However, if you begin to see that your expenses are growing faster than your salary and you have to dip into your savings to pay your monthly bills, you are now in deficit spending. Your personal finances, in this instance, parallel those of school districts. If school district revenues exceed expenditures year after year, the district is quite solvent. However, once their expenditures begin exceeding revenues on a regular basis, the district too has a deficit problem.

As an individual you have, of course, several realistic options to eliminate your personal deficit. First, you could cut your expenses. This approach, however, may mean that you cannot do some of the things to which you have become accustomed. You may have to go out to dinner less often, postpone a vacation, or keep your present car a few years longer. You could also look for a new position with a higher salary or consider supplementing your income by taking a part-time job. Some combination of these strategies may solve your personal deficit spending problem.

School districts, on the other hand, have a very similar problem but without many of the options available to you. Similar to your personal finances, when school district revenues fail to keep up with expenditures, school administrators and school boards must increase revenues and/or cut expenditures. They will need to use their cash reserves just as you might tap into your savings account to cover immediate shortfalls.

As you will see shortly, the most significant difference between individuals and school districts is that school districts have fewer options primarily on the revenue side to solve their financial problems than do individuals. Also, school boards must conduct their business in public view while subject, at times, to an uninformed and sometimes angry public and special interest groups. The political nature of school governance at the state and school board levels is a challenge which individuals do not typically face. Yet, once you understand the basic revenue/expenditure principle of state and local school district finances, much of the mystery of school finance will disappear.

Chapter 2

Historical Basis for Public School Funding

Before considering school district finances, it is important to understand why the federal government plays such a small role in public education. It is equally important to understand what role it does play. Let's begin with some questions.

- Do you know why state legislators, rather the federal government, seem so much more involved in public education?
- Have you ever lived in another state with just a handful of county-wide school districts and wondered why some states such as Illinois have hundreds of school districts, some with as few as a hundred or two hundred students?
- Have you noticed that certain states have had their funding systems ruled unconstitutional while a state such as Illinois with a tremendous variance in the amount spent per pupil between the wealthy and poorer school districts is allowed to continue as is?

The answer to these central questions requires a very basic understanding of the legal authority for public education.

LEGAL AUTHORITY FOR PUBLIC EDUCATION

Shortly after this country was founded, the U. S. Constitution was written establishing the legal authority for public education. The key section was the tenth amendment which states that, "The powers not delegated to the United States by the Constitution, nor prohibited by it to the States, are reserved to the States, or to the people." (Yudof, Kirp & Levin, 1992, p. 841). Through this amendment, our founding fathers delegated to the states, not the federal government, the legal authority for the governance of public education. Ultimately, states created their own unique public education systems through their individual state constitutions. As a result, even though public education systems are similar from state to state, the delegation of the responsibility for public education to the states has meant that each is at liberty to design its own public education system within the parameters of federal law.

Does this mean that the federal government has no role in public education? Far from it. Although the federal government does not have direct control over public education, it is not without influence. However, because of the tenth amendment, its influence has historically been less than that of state government.

ROLE OF THE FEDERAL GOVERNMENT

Since the federal government has no direct authority for public education, its primary mode of action is to pass legislation often linked directly to federal funding. In essence, national political leaders create public policy by tying initiatives to federal dollars. States and more specifically school districts that want federal funding are required to meet certain federal requirements. This formula approach has proven to be a particularly effective way for federal policy-makers to influence public education on a national level.

KEY FEDERAL INITIATIVES

To further understand how the federal government influences public education, let's take a brief look at four historic federal educational initiatives. Although a discussion of all federal initiatives is impractical and unnecessary, understanding these which have substantially impacted the development of American public education and to some degree educational funding will provide valuable insights into how the federal government uses dollars to influence public education policy and programming.

LAND ORDINANCE OF 1785

A landmark piece of federal legislation, the Land Ordinance of 1785, is one of these initiatives (Brimley & Garfield, 2002). Adopted by the Continental Congress on May 20, 1785, it had several purposes; however, one of its key provisions was to divide the land acquired from Britain following the Revolutionary War, primarily in the Midwest, into six mile square townships, each composed of 36 one square mile blocks (See Table 2.1 below). Depending upon natural factors such as rivers, the size of the actual township could vary. The federal governmental then sold many of these sections to raise capital, in part, to re-pay war debt. However, a unique provision of the Act was the requirement that Section 16 of the thirty-six mile square block be set aside for the maintenance of public schools. Many of these were sold to raise revenue for public education. Additional land ordinance legislation called the Northwest Ordinance was passed in 1787. It included the phrase, "...religion, morality, and knowledge being necessary to good government and the happiness of mankind, schools and the means of school shall be forever encouraged." This gave further impetus to establishing a priority for public education in areas beyond the original thirteen states and also a property basis for school funding (Alexander & Alexander, 2005, p.1019).

Table 2.1
Township Grid

1	2	3	4	5	6
7	8	9	10	11	12
13	14	15	16	17	18
19	20	21	22	13	24
25	26	27	28	29	30
31	32	33	34	35	36

Think for a moment how this Act is reflected in Illinois even today. As an Illinois resident, you can probably identify the township in which you live. If not, you will likely find the township listed on your property tax bill. To understand how the township system still impacts Illinois public schools, let us use Niles Township as an example. The township is composed of the following elementary (K-8) school districts:

- Golf School District 67
- Skokie School District 68
- Skokie School District 69
- Morton Grove School District 70
- Niles School District 71
- Fairview School District 72
- East Prairie School District 73
- Skokie School District 73 ½
- Lincolnwood School District 74

With the exception of a small portion of Golf 67 that was annexed to Glenview Consolidated School District 34 in the 1980s, all school district boundaries are coterminous (same boundaries) with Niles Township High School District 219, which is the public high school district serving all township students. You may note the use of the term township in the name of the high school district.

This township pattern is common in Illinois, although outside the suburban Chicago area, many school districts are actually unit (K-12) districts. Over the years, various school district consolidation efforts and other factors have altered the original pattern in some areas of the state. However, the importance of the Land Ordinance of 1785 on the growth and funding of public schools cannot be underestimated.

FEDERAL VOCATIONAL EDUCATION ACT

In 1917, federal legislation entitled the Federal Vocational Education Act, sometimes referred to as the Smith-Hughes Act, became law. For the first time, federal funds were used to support the development of pre-collegiate courses in vocational education and related teacher training. By earmarking these funds, the federal government supported the development of public school vocational education programs throughout the country (Guthrie, 2003). This is a good example of how the federal government uses dollars to promote a specific educational initiative without the legal authority to mandate it.

ELEMENTARY AND SECONDARY EDUCATION ACT OF 1965 (ESEA)

A more recent and sweeping example of a federal policy is the Elementary and Secondary Education Act of 1965 which was originally signed into law by President Lyndon B. Johnson in 1965. A central component of Johnson's War on Poverty, ESEA was designed to assist primarily economically disadvantaged students through funding a variety of federal programs. ESEA was divided into various sections called Titles. One of the most well known was Title I: Improving the Academic Achievement of the Disadvantaged. Title I, a federal grant program, was created to improve the reading and mathematics achievement of children from lower socioeconomic backgrounds. School districts seeking federal Title I funding must provide certain types student services and follow grant guidelines to be eligible. Most school districts continue to receive federal Title I dollars even today (Beyer & Johnson, 2005).

Since 1965, ESEA has been periodically reauthorized, each time reflecting the educational policy agenda of the federal government at the time. You will undoubtedly recognize the most recent reauthorization – No Child Left Behind (Beyer & Johnson, 2005).

EDUCATION OF ALL HANDICAPPED CHILDREN ACT OF 1975 (PUBLIC LAW 94-142)

One of my most vivid teaching memories from the early 1970s is trying to teach language arts in an affluent suburban Chicago school district in heterogeneous classes of twenty-five plus students. In each class, I had some students who were academically gifted and a few who could barely read and write beyond a primary grade level. As an English major trained primary in the greatest works of literature, I had very little preparation to teach low functioning students in my language arts class. As a beginning teacher, I decided to approach our school counselors for advice. I assumed that either they would be able to provide me with advice or recommend a veteran teacher who could mentor me.

After I explained the difficulties I was having and asked for advice, I remember how the counselor, a very experienced faculty member, leaned back in his desk chair while smoking his pipe and offered me his sage advice. He began by saying that there are just some students who are like this. He said that he did not have any specific suggestions other than to do the best I could with these children. I was amazed by his comments. Surely, another faculty member must have had success with needy students. As I asked other teachers, I received the same advice.

What I realized later was that special education was in its infancy. Our school, which was in a very progressive district, had only one Educationally Mentally Handicapped (EMH) classroom and two resource tutors who periodically pulled students from class for individual reading support. I remember a year later hearing about an area special education cooperative but knew almost nothing about it. So was the state of special education in the early '70s.

Then along came PL 94-142, Educational of all Handicapped Children Act. The passage of this federal legislation guaranteed for the first time a free, appropriate public education to each child with disabilities (United States Department of Education, 2007). The rest, of course, is history. Beginning with this federal legislation which includes funding support, the growth of special education programs and services has been dramatic. Today this is probably the most far reaching and extensive federal policy initiative impacting public education.

SUMMARY

In Chapter 2, we examined the legal basis for our system of public education including the impact of the 10th amendment. We also studied four examples of historic federal legislation to understand how the federal government uses its resources to influence affect people's lives through public education policy and programming even without direct constitutional authority.

Chapter 3

Sources of Revenue

Now that we have taken a brief look at the legal basis for public education and examined the role of the federal government, let us turn our attention to the first side of the basic finance equation – sources of revenue; or more specifically, where school districts find the dollars to operate. Overall, school districts rely on several primary revenue sources including:

- Property taxes;
- General State Aid;
- Poverty Grant;
- Categorical State Aid;
- Competitive grants;
- Corporate Personal Property Replacement Tax (CPPRT);
- Interest income;
- Local fees; and,
- Federal aid.

PROPERTY TAXES

I am sure that you would not be surprised to hear that the largest single source of Illinois public education funding is the property tax. In fact, in fiscal year 2009, local sources of revenue which are primarily property taxes comprised 56.2% of all public school revenues in Illinois (Illinois State Board of Education, 2012a). Note: In school finance, fiscal year refers to a traditional school year July 1 to June 30. Therefore, FY 13 is July 1, 2012 through June 30, 2013. For some school districts, primarily in the northeast portion of the state, property taxes are the most substantial revenue source accounting for more than half of their total revenues. However, for other school districts with lower property tax bases, the impact of property taxes may be somewhat less than other revenue sources since their property tax bases provide a smaller portion of overall school district revenues. Also not surprising, some districts with low property wealth, such as those in rural areas, experience little if any property value growth from year to year.

TAX BASE

A school district's wealth is usually linked to the total value of taxable property within district boundaries. This is what is called the tax base. A school district's tax base is determined by adding together the value of all taxable property whether it is vacant land, residential, or business-based. Since the value of property varies depending on its location and type, some school districts will have much more property wealth than others.

For example, if your school district is located in the northern suburbs of Chicago and includes a regional shopping mall and multiple high-rise corporate office buildings, your overall tax base will be dramatically higher than in a farming community in Livingston County. Because of such wide discrepancies in Illinois school district tax bases, a great deal of inequity exists between the highest and lowest wealth school districts.

TAX EXEMPT PROPERTY

Some property owners do not pay property taxes because the property is tax exempt. Examples of common tax exempt properties include those occupied by governmental units such as military bases, municipal and state offices, and legally designated not-for-profits such as places of worship, some hospitals, universities, and other organizations. For many school districts, tax exempt properties are a small percentage of the overall tax base. But in others, such as Evanston Community Consolidated School District 65 which includes Northwestern University, a significant portion of property is not taxed and is unavailable for other development thereby reducing the school district's property tax base.

UNDERSTANDING THE PROPERTY TAX IN ILLINOIS

Before considering issues surrounding property taxes, it is important to understand how property taxes are calculated. Theoretically, calculations for all taxable property in Illinois should, by law, be based on one-third of the property's market value (actual selling price) (Fritts, 2008). Therefore, if your home has a market value of $600,000, it should be assessed for tax calculation purposes at 1/3 or $200,000. This $200,000 is called the assessed valuation. All Illinois counties including Cook are supposed to tax property based on one-third of market value. However, here is where Cook County differs from the rest of the state. Cook County, instead of assessing all property at 33%, uses a tiered system, which assesses business property at a higher rate than residential property.

Let's examine this a little closer. In Cook County, homeowners' property should be assessed at 16% of market value and businesses between 33% and 38%, depending upon the type of business entity (Illinois Department of Revenue, 2012). However, beginning with 2009 taxes received in 2010, Cook County residential property will be assessed at ten percent and commercial property at twenty-five percent (Houlihan, 2009).

In all other counties, both homeowners and businesses are assessed at 33%. The figure below shows the legal assessment percentages.

Table 3.1
County Tax Assessment Levels

Tax Payer	Cook County	Other Counties
Homeowner	10%	33%
Businesses	25%	33%

This multi-tiered assessment system in Cook County was designed to reduce homeowner property taxes. In essence, businesses pay a higher percentage of the overall taxes to allow homeowners to pay less.

The concept of fixed assessment levels for property tax purposes seems logical and fair. If all Illinois real estate was assessed according to the mandated formula, the system would appear to be fair since everyone would be treated consistently. However, have you ever compared your tax bill with a neighbor, perhaps even with someone who has the same model home in your subdivision, and wondered why that person's tax bill was different from yours? If so, you are not alone.

PROPERTY ASSESSMENT INCONSISTENCIES

To understand why this occurs, it is important to recognize that assessment of property is not an exact science. In Illinois, county property tax assessors oversee the assessment and reassessment of all property in their respective counties. As with any such process, the assessment process is somewhat subjective since it relies on individuals who have some discretion to interpret information and make judgments. As a result, property assessments vary from area to area from year to year.

In addition, Cook County property has been historically under-assessed. Recent studies of actual assessment levels show these discrepancies. Fritts (2008) reports that residential property is actually assessed at 10% of fair market value and business property in a range of 27-30%. In part, because of these underassessment practices, the Cook County Board recently revised the Real Property Assessment Classification Ordinance to set residential assessment at 10% and business/commercial at 25% beginning with 2009 assessments (Herman & Kownacki, 2008).

To adjust for some of the assessment variance from county to county, the state created a balancing system called the State Equalization Factor.

STATE EQUALIZATION FACTOR

The State Equalization Factor or as it is commonly called the "Multiplier" is a factor assigned to a county to bring the average county-wide property assessment level to the required one-third (Illinois Department of Revenue, 2011). If a county is under-assessing, the state can eliminate some of the discrepancy by increasing the multiplier.

Here is how it works. When property in a given county is correctly assessed at one-third of its market value, the state assigns a multiplier of 1.0. On the other hand, when property in a county is under-assessed, the state assigns the county a higher multiplier which is applied equally to all property in the county. The multiplier is supposed to bring the overall assessment of property in the county to the one-third standard. For example, the state assigned a multiplier of 2.9706 for Cook County for Tax Year 2011 because both residential and business/commercial properties were under assessed.

The table below demonstrates the different assessment levels in Cook and Lake Counties. It also shows how the multiplier is used to bring property assessments to the mandated level. You will note that businesses in Cook are assessed at a significantly higher than residential property. Also by applying the multiplier, the state has attempted to bring the total county-wide property assessment in Cook to 33% of the total market value.

Table 3.2
Effect of Multiplier

County	Market Value	Assessed Value	Multiplier	*Equalized Assessed Value*
Lake-Home	$600,000	$200,000	1	*$200,000*
Lake-Business	$600,000	$200,000	1	*$200,000*
Cook-Home	$600,000	$60,000	2.9786	*$178,716*
Cook-Business	$600,000	$150,000	2.9786	*$446,790*

EQUALIZED ASSESSED VALUATION (EAV)

In the figure above, you may have noticed that I introduced a new term, Equalized Assessed Valuation (EAV). Since assessment levels may vary from county to county, in particular from Cook, the property tax calculation you will see shortly requires that assessed values be converted to EAV as part of the property tax calculation process. So when you hear EAV, be aware that this is the revised assessed value of the home after the state multiplier has been applied to adjust for under-assessment.

FURTHER EXEMPTIONS

If calculating property taxes was not complicated enough, the state legislature has created several special tax exemptions designed to reduce property taxes for specific groups (Illinois Department of Revenue, 2011). These "exempt" a portion of the EAV from the property tax calculation thereby reducing taxes for that particular property. The most common exemptions in Illinois are:
- Homestead (An exemption for owners of primary residences);
- Senior Homestead (Additional exemption for seniors); and,
- Disabled Veterans.

In addition, low income seniors who meet certain eligibility requirements qualify for a Senior Citizen Assessment Freeze. Later in this chapter, we will examine a sample property tax bill which will include some of these exemptions.

So far we have discussed several factors which are used in the property tax calculation: market value, assessed valuation, equalized assessed valuation (EAV), and exemptions. The last factor you need to understand is tax rate.

TAX RATE

The most confusing term in the property tax formula is the tax rate which is the percentage at which property is taxed. State laws regulate tax rates. However, for most individuals other than school business officials and superintendents, what is most important to know is not how the tax rate is calculated but rather how it is applied to individual taxpayer bills. Since the imposition of the tax cap in Illinois and recent legislation, the tax rate has become a less important factor for school districts. Tax rate will be discussed further later.

PROPERTY TAX FORMULA

Now that we have examined the factors that are used in the property tax calculation, we can now apply the formula. Although the mathematical calculation is quite simple, it often appears confusing unless you understand the factors. I like to tell graduate students that the actual math problem could easily be completed by many third graders! What makes the formula particularly confusing is that the tax rate is applied for every one hundred dollars of EAV not total EAV. The property tax formula is:

- Individual Property Owner's EAV/100 X Total Tax Rate = Total Property Tax Bill
- To understand this calculation, let's consider a specific example of a typical home. Our assumptions are:
  (a) Home has an EAV of $50,000 (Market value of $150,000) and
  (b) The total tax rate for all taxing bodies is $6.00.

Here is the calculation:

> **Step 1:** Take the EAV and divide it by 100. The formula says that the tax rate is applied to every $100 of EAV not the total amount. Therefore, you must calculate how many hundreds of dollars of EAV you have.

> $50,000/100 = $500

> **Step 2:** Multiple this number by the tax rate. In reality, the property owner is paying $6.00 in property taxes on every 100 of EAV.

> $500 X $6.00 = $3,000

It is that simple! What confuses everyone is how you arrive at the tax rate and how you calculate the final EAV.

UNDERSTANDING A TAX BILL

Have you ever studied your own property tax bill? You have probably looked at the bottom line, compared various figures from the current to last year's but never really took time to understand it. Yet, one of the best ways to understand property taxes is to examine an actual property tax bill. The basic components of property tax bills are common in all counties. However, because Cook County is different in some respects, we will examine a sample Cook County tax bill (See Sample Cook County Tax Bill below).

To begin, you will note that this is the second installment, which is due in the fall. In the bottom right hand corner, you will find the amount paid in the first installment, $4,984.72, and second, $3,776.75. The total property taxes due on this residential property for the year are $8,761.41.

COOK COUNTY TAX CALCULATION

This bill illustrates how Cook County property taxes are billed differently from the remainder of the state. This taxpayer paid $9,063.12 in tax year 2008. The first installment due for tax year 2009 was 55% of the previous year's total bill, $4,984.72. Since the first installment is due earlier in Cook than other counties, the exact annual property tax is unknown at the time so 55% of the prior year's amount is billed. The second installment is $3,776.75 which reflects the difference between the first installment and the total actual property taxes due after property tax calculations are completed.

Figure 3.1. Sample Cook County Tax Bill

YEAR IN ARREARS

When you hear that property taxes are always billed a year behind, this is because they are assessed in one year, in this case 2009, and actually paid in the next, 2010. This bill provides an example of this process, which often causes some confusion when trying to explain property taxes.

Adding further to possible misinterpretation is the difference between tax year and fiscal year. In the Sample Tax Bill above, the tax year is January 1 to December 31 and is different from fiscal year which is always July 1 to June 30.

REASSESSMENT PRACTICES

The 2009 Assessed Value is $57,283. This can remain the same from one year to the next if it is not a reassessment year. Cook County property is reassessed every three years.

In other counties, state statute requires that individual properties be reviewed every four years. However, it is common for townships in these counties to review the fair market value of properties annually against assessment levels sometimes resulting in the application of a township equalizer.

TAXING DISTRICTS

The tax bill also identifies the taxing bodies legally authorized to levy property taxes. On the sample bill, both the elementary and high school districts collect the majority of property taxes. One interesting point to remember is that taxing bodies are not required to levy taxes. In non-election years, for example, no taxes are typically collected for "Consolidated Elections."

TAX RATES

As mentioned earlier, tax rate are very confusing particularly since the property tax cap became law in such counties as Cook. What actually occurs is that the tax rate is calculated after the amount of property taxes a district is entitled to under law is determined and the overall EAV within the boundaries of the taxing body is established. The tax rate is then set at the level needed to generate the amount of property taxes the taxing body is requesting as long as the rate does not exceed the maximum permitted by law. If it does, then the tax rate is reduced to the legal limit and the taxing body does not receive all the property taxes requested. This is one of the reasons that school districts ask the voters to approve a tax increase through a referendum.

TAX CALCULATOR

Earlier we discussed the formula used to calculate a property owner's tax liability. In summary, the EAV of the property is divided by 100 and multiplied by the tax rate to establish the total property taxes due for the year. You can understand this process by examining the information listed under Tax Calculator on right side of the sample tax bill.

2008 Assessed Value. This represents the value assigned to the property by the county assessor for the prior tax year.

2009 Assessed Value. This line should be the projected value of the home if it was sold.

2009 Assessed Value. This figure represents the assessed value based on the county assessor's calculation for this tax year. If you simple multiple the property value, $572,830, by 10%, you have an assessed value of $57,283.

2009 State Equalization Factor. If the Cook County Assessor had calculated the assessed value of residential property at approximately the 16% level, the multiplier would close to 1.0. However, since the state through an analysis process determined that the assessor undervalued property, the state assigned a higher "multiplier" to attempt to equalize the low assessed value. Since the state has assigned the county a multiplier of 3.3701, the property was substantially under assessed in relationship to other counties.

2009 Tax Rate and 2009 Total Tax before Exemptions. Now that the EAV is set, the actual tax calculation can occur. The County Clerk divides the EAV, $193.049 by 100 which equals $1,930.49 and then multiplies this figure by the tax rate of 5.063 which yields a Tax Year 2009 (payable in 2010) bill of $9,774.07.

Tax Exemption. In Illinois, certain taxpayers are provided some property tax relief through the legislative process. This particular homeowner received a Homeowner's Exemption of $1,012.60. Most homeowners have a Homeowners Exemption and receive a reduction in property taxes due to a reduction made in the EAV.

2009 Total Tax after Exemptions. To arrive at the final property tax bill, the homeowner exemption amount is deducted from the amount listed under Property Tax before Exemptions which determines the total property taxes paid in 2010. For this property, this was $8,761.47.

In other counties, the homeowner exemption may be stated as an amount of EAV which is deducted from the total EAV rather than a dollar amount. In any event, they both reduce the taxpayer's property taxes.

What never ceases to amaze me is just how complicated the formula appears to be. However, when you understand each of the parts, the actual calculation is quite simple. The real challenge for school administrators and school board members is to explain this process to citizens and employees in a way that they understand the calculation but also appreciate the issues and political factors which have and continue to play a role in this process over time, particularly since any major revision is not imminent.

TAX COLLECTION TIMELINE

School districts submit their property tax levy to the county by the last Tuesday in December. The tax levy is the specific dollar amount in property taxes that the school district requests. We will examine further how the levy is determined when we discuss the Illinois tax cap.

Property taxes are collected twice a year and distributed to taxing bodies as they are received. School districts typically receive their first property tax payments in the spring. Since these arrive before the beginning of the school year for which they are intended, they are referred to as early taxes.

Early taxes can be a source of confusion for some school districts. For example, if your district is in the process of contract negotiations and receives $3,000,000 in early taxes, the teachers' union may argue that the district has an additional $3,000,000 in reserves. The school board may counter that this is not part of the carryover reserve, but only a temporary increase in the reserve because the funds are actually for the next school year.

One other confusing property tax issue is how Cook County residential spring property tax bills are calculated. School districts have to request property taxes in December before they know how much they are entitled to receive. The county clerk's office determines the exact level later in the spring. Because Cook County tax bills are distributed before the process is completed, the Cook County Clerk bills the property owner for 55% of the last year's tax. Then, in the fall after all pertinent data have been received, the actual full-year tax bill is calculated. The difference between what the property owner paid in the first installment and what is outstanding is the amount the property owner is billed for the fall installment. This is why the second half property tax bill may be higher or lower than the first. Since other counties distribute the first tax bill later than in Cook, usually in June, this is not an issue for the counties as the total property tax bill is divided equally between the two payments.

GENERAL STATE AID

A second source of revenue is General State Aid (GSA) that is distributed based on a formula. The operating principle behind the Illinois' general state aid formulas is this. School districts that have the least local wealth should receive the most GSA. This is, in concept, an equity principle. The Illinois State Board of Education uses a worksheet which school district administrators complete to establish their level of local wealth. For the most part, local wealth is tied to EAV per pupil. The higher the EAV is per pupil; the wealthier the school district.

In theory, by providing increased state aid to less wealthy school districts, the inequity gap in overall spending per pupil between property wealthy and property poor school districts should be reduced. I say in theory because, as you will soon see, state aid does not come close to accomplishing this.

FOUNDATION LEVEL

The first step in establishing General State Aid is for the legislature and governor to set a foundation level. This represents the minimum guaranteed amount of funding per student including local and state funds deemed necessary to educate a child in Illinois (Center for Tax and Budget Accountability, 2009). For FY 2012, this figure was $6,119 per student. See table below for a recent history of the foundation level (Illinois State Board of Education, 2012a).

Table 3.3
Recent History of the Foundation Level

Year	Level
FY 2002	$4,560
FY 2003	$4,560
FY 2004	$4,810
FY 2005	$4,964
FY 2006	$5,164
FY 2007	$5,334
FY 2008	$5,734
FY 2009	$5,959
FY 2010	$6,119
FY 2011	$6,119
FY 2012	$6,119

The foundation level is important since the Illinois State Board of Education uses it as a factor in the general state aid calculation.

STATE AID FORMULAS

Once the foundation level is established for the fiscal year, it is used as a factor in determining under which of the three state aid formulas a school district receives General State Aid funding. School districts qualify for funding based upon their local wealth per student as measured against the foundation level for the coming year.

The first is the Foundation Formula or as it is sometimes called the Resource Equalizer. Do not confuse foundation level with Foundation Formula even though they use similar terms. School districts that have low local revenues qualify for funding under the Foundation Formula. Since these districts are below the basic state-identified foundation level minimum, they are by definition the least wealthy school districts in Illinois. Consequently, they receive the most General State Aid. For FY 2012, 625 school districts were funded under the Foundation Formula (Illinois State Board of Education, 2012c).

For those school districts whose local revenues are slightly higher but do not have enough local property tax support, the ISBE assigns them to the Alternate Method. These school districts (171) receive less GSA than the least wealthy school districts but more than the wealthiest school (Illinois State Board of Education, 2012c).

School districts that have more substantial local funding receive the least GSA. Most of these 69 school districts are in northeast Illinois where property values are significantly higher than other areas of the state. These school districts qualify for what is termed the Flat Grant method. These districts receive a "flat" $218 per student. This figure has remained constant for many years as most general state aid increases have been directed at the needier school districts (Illinois State Board of Education, 2012c).

POVERTY GRANT STATE FUNDING

In addition to GSA, all school districts receive Poverty Grant Funding, which is designed to provide school districts with additional state aid for low income students. The amount of funding received is calculated under a separate statutory formula based on Illinois Department of Human Services (DHS) populations or benefit recipients that includes a three year average of the unduplicated count of district students who qualify for Medicaid or food stamps. School districts with 15% or less qualifying students receive a flat $355 per student. Over 15%, the amount of funding provided increases based on the percentage of qualifying students. The formula is often described as curvilinear since the rate of per pupil funding increases more as the percentage of low income students increases.

Poverty Grant Funding, though, is not equity-based. The formula does not include consideration of local district wealth but only the low income student count. As a result, even wealthy school districts receive the same level of funding as the least wealthy if they have the same percentage of qualifying students. In fact, some school districts, especially those under the flat grant formula, may actually receive more Poverty Grant Funding than GSA.

EDUCATIONAL FUNDING ADVISORY BOARD

In 1997, Illinois established the Educational Funding Advisory Board (EFAB), which is composed of representatives from business, education, and the public. EFAB is primarily responsible for recommending an annual minimum foundation level tied to the actual cost of providing students an adequate education. "Adequate" is defined as an amount necessary to ensure that at least 67% of non-at-risk students achieve a passing test score on Illinois' standardized achievement test. Initially, EFAB worked with a nationally recognized consulting firm to create a formula designed to achieve the goal of providing a minimum level of public school funding needed for an "adequate" education while ensuring that the spending levels of wealthier school districts did not inflate this foundation figure. When the formula was developed, EFAB included an inflation factor, which was tied to the Employment Cost Index and designed to adjust the foundation level automatically each year (Center for Tax and Budget Accountability, 2009).

Unfortunately, due primarily to a lack of revenues, the state has never fully funded EFAB recommendations. In fact, the state typically sets the foundation level well below that deemed necessary by EFAB and has never implemented the inflation adjustment process (Center for Tax and Budget Accountability, 2009).

STATE AID ISSUES

Earlier, I mentioned that state aid does not actually close the gap between wealthy and poorer school districts. Let's examine some of the issues related to state aid that impact school districts.

Inadequate Foundation Level

Do you think that your school district can adequately educate a child on the FY 2011 foundation level of $6,119? Not likely since the average operating expense per pupil expenditure in Illinois for FY09 was $11,197 (a, 2012). Such a low funding level would mean huge class sizes, few non-essential courses, low paid employees, and more.

So why not raise the foundation level to the point that the poorest districts are on par with the wealthiest? Simply, the state does not have the resources to do so. The dollars needed would be so high that it would be economically unfeasible. To put this in perspective, Illinois public schools enrolled 2,074,806 students in FY 2011 (Illinois State Board of Education, 2012a). If the state contributed merely $1,000 more per student, this would require approximately $2.1B initially in additional state funding.

As a result, the foundation level continues to increase slowly from year to year (See Table 3.3) without closing the inequity gap. However, what many hope is that the legislature will approve some substantial increase in general state aid for school districts which qualify under the Foundation Formula and the Alternative Method formulas. They may not achieve equity with Flat Grant districts, but they would receive much needed additional revenues without negatively affecting the Flat Grant districts which are fixed at $218 per pupil.

Categorical State Aid

In additional to general state aid which is available for a wide range of expenditures, school districts receive categorical state aid funding, which is most often targeted at special need students and programs. As distinguished from competitive grants, school districts do not compete for categorical aid. Rather, those districts that meet specific requirements and complete the necessary paperwork receive funding. Examples of Illinois categorical state aid programs for FY 2012 were (Illinois State Board of Education, 2012a):

- Special Education Personnel;
- Special Education Transportation;
- Special Education Private Tuition;
- Regular Transportation;
- Bilingual Education;
- Regular Education Orphanage; and,
- Free Breakfast/Lunch.

School districts submit their state categorical grant applications in the summer and generally receive payments quarterly during the fiscal year.

Categorical state aid is an important source of revenue for school districts, even those with high per pupil spending. In fact, flat grant districts unusually receive more actual dollars per student in categorical than general state aid. Therefore, categorical aid is quite important to these wealthier districts as well.

Prorating of Categorical Aid

Historically, in a poor state economy, Illinois is short on revenues. Does this sound familiar today? Consequently, one strategy that the state employs in tough financial times is to prorate categorical funding; that is, provide school districts with only a percentage of the categorical funding they are entitled to receive. For example, if Illinois decides to short change, or prorate, special education funding to 90%, a school district entitled to $200,000 would only receive $180,000. Prorating categorical funding can create a level of uncertainty which most affects those less wealthy districts which are more state aid dependent and most need state revenue.

Politics

One of the most substantial benefits of property taxes is they are not subject to the state political process and partisan politics. When a school district requests property taxes to which it is entitled, it receives almost its entire request. However, local politics can play a part in determining local school district property tax revenue.

Each year the school board must pass a tax levy, a board action authorizing a specific dollar amount in property taxes for which the school district has the legal authority to request. The exact amount a district can receive is defined in state law. However, boards of education must follow legally defined procedures which include providing notice to the public and conducting a public hearing, if levy is 5% or higher than the previous year, before they can request a specific tax levy amount (Braun, 2010). Through this process, interested citizens have the opportunity to address the board. As such, taxpayers can pressure school boards to levy less than what the district is entitled under the law.

I remember a meeting during which sixty senior citizens packed our school board meeting to attempt to pressure the board to lower its tax levy. Administrators must be prepared to respond to this type pressure in the present anti-tax political climate.

While politics play only a minimal role with property taxes, the same cannot be said of state aid. School districts which rely heavily on general state aid (Foundation Formula and Alternative Method districts) are most affected by the annual Springfield legislative process. In recent years during which state revenues have been relatively flat as the state economy weakened, K-12 educators have often found themselves in competition with other state agencies such as public assistance, mental health, and transportation for a share of a finite state revenue pool. Recently, public education has fared reasonably well through this process with annual general state aid increases. However, the reality is that there is one pie and many groups vying for a bigger slice!

In contrast, flat grant districts which receive only $218 in general state aid and often spend more than $10,000 per student care a great deal more about property taxes than general state aid (Illinois State Board of Education, 2012a). The Foundation Level really has little real impact on them because they are not as state aid dependent.

As you can probably surmise from above, general state aid is much more important to Foundation Formula and Alternative Method than Flat Grant school districts.

Another equally important economic and political issue is categorical state aid funding. Since all school districts even those under the Flat Grant formula receive these state funds, school boards and administrators must pay particular attention to legislative discussions on categorical funding levels. All school districts share a common interest in categorical funding.

Finally, since Illinois is such a diverse state, where your school district is located, how dependent you are on state aid, whether you are a large unit, suburban, urban, or rural school district, or, for that matter, the Chicago Public School system, you may have common or conflicting school funding interests with other school districts. As a result, individual school districts or groups of districts traditionally advocate for their personal needs through the state political process.

Both state legislators and governors, all of whom are elected officials and hope to retain their positions, must find some way to walk this political tightrope. As a result, they are often reluctant to favor one group position at the expense of another. Consequently, those seeking their share of state revenues must not only lobby the legislature and governor regularly for additional funding but often fight to maintain the level of support they already have.

CORPORATE PERSONAL PROPERTY REPLACEMENT TAX (CPPRT)

Another source of school district revenue is CPPRT, which was initiated following the abolition of the Illinois Personal Property Tax when the Illinois Constitution was revised in 1970. Unless you are a school business official, you really only need to understand that CPPRT is a state tax on either income or invested capital, on some businesses to replace lost revenue from the abolition of the personal property tax on corporations, partnerships, and other business entities (Illinois Department of Revenue, 2012). School districts receive money from state-collected CPPRT taxes each year. Usually, school districts are notified of their estimated CPPRT amount in the summer and receive payments throughout the year. The amount generally increases annually but can also decrease. For some school districts, this can be significant resource revenue. An economic downturn can negatively affect this revenue source. Since school districts have no control over the tax, they merely include CPPRT funds as revenue in their budgets.

SALES TAX REVENUE

Until recently, no school boards were able to generate sales tax revenue. However, a few years ago the legislature passed Public Act 95-675, which allows all counties except Cook to levy a 1% sales tax for school facility purposes through referendum. Revenues received are allocated to schools based on the enrollment of students living in the county (Local Governments' Guide to Tax, 2012). Because of the required referendum process, approving a school facilities sales tax in many counties is unfeasible. Most counties, including those in the Chicago area have never even asked voters for approval. However, the following counties have passed the sales tax: Cass, Champaign, Franklin, Jo Daviess, Knox, Laurence, Logan, Macon, Saline, Schuyler, Warren, and Williamson. The tax was rejected by voters in 22 other counties including Macoupin, Madison, and Sangamon. Other counties have yet to put the referendum before voters. Nonetheless, this revenue option is another potential source of school funding.

COMPETITIVE GRANTS

Similar to the federal government, state public officials will use specific initiatives to promote their policy agendas. For example, a recent Illinois governor proposed providing all day kindergarten and reducing primary class size. Rather than distributing funding to all school districts which is not realistic due to limited availability of state funds, he initiated a competitive grant program. Some school districts competed against each other for a fixed pool of dollars.

For some school districts, particularly those with limited revenue, competitive grants, which may include those from private sources, may be an important source of funding. Competitive grants may mean the difference between either offering or not providing much needed programs in cash-strapped school districts.

However, school districts must be careful to ensure that a competitive grant makes educational and financial sense. You may want to ask yourself the following questions when you are considering applying for a competitive grant. How you respond to these will help you decide whether a particular competitive grant is appropriate for your school district.

- Does the purpose of the grant align with district needs?
- Does the grant require the district to provide additional funding?
- How will the faculty and parents react if a grant-funded program is discontinued after two or three years?
- How will the district maintain a grant-based program after funding is discontinued?

FEDERAL AID

Illinois, similar to other states, receives substantial federal education funding. For FY 12, the federal government contributed $3,460.8 billion or 12.3% percent of Illinois

Sources of Revenue

K-12 public school revenues (Illinois State Board of Education, 2012a). These funds are distributed by the federal government to states where they are disbursed primarily as categorical grants to school districts. Examples of the major federal categorical grants include the Federal Lunch Program and ESEA (No Child Left Behind) Title programs. School districts with larger economically disadvantaged student populations generally receive a higher proportion of need-based federal funding. In addition, the federal government also uses a competitive grant process to promote particular initiatives. The United States Department of Education includes competitive grant information on its website at www.ed.gov. Although federal funding for almost all Illinois school districts is not as substantial a source of school district revenue as are property taxes and state aid, it is none-the-less important for all school districts in this era of limited revenues and rising expenditures.

LOCAL SOURCES

School districts also collect a variety of local user-based fees throughout the school year. Although most of the amounts are relatively small, the revenue is important in times of revenue shortfalls and ever increasing expenditures. Fee increases in financially strapped school districts are often viewed by those without children in school as a preferable option to increase revenues since those who benefit directly are only affected. Local funding sources generally include fees that are established annually by the board of education on the recommendation of the administration.

- School textbook, yearbook, and activity fees (athletic and extracurricular);
- Breakfast and lunch program fees;
- Bus fees;
- Student fines;
- Student technology fees;
- Other program fees such as summer school or after school childcare; and,
- Building rental fees.

INTEREST INCOME

One source of revenue which you may not have considered is investment income. School districts always maintain some reserve funds for cash flow purposes to ensure that they have sufficient dollars available to pay bills and meet their payrolls while waiting for state aid and property tax revenues to arrive. Everyone from individuals to businesses usually have some funds in reserve at any given time.

Laws govern where school districts can invest reserve funds and how they can be used. However, in general, reserves must be kept in low risk, reasonably accessible short-term financial investment vehicles such as certificates of deposit and government securities, many of which yield interest income (Braun, 2010). School districts with substantial reserves often generate significant interest revenue that can be used to pay

operating expenses. In Illinois, investment options are more conservative than in some other states. For districts with large reserves and current operating budget deficits, interest revenue is very important part of the revenue stream.

Although interest income is an important revenue source, a budget deficit can dramatically impact its effectiveness. When a school district is in deficit spending, the dollars needed to make up the deficit come from reserves. As a result, when the school district draws down its reserve to offset a budget deficit, not only does the district have fewer reserves, but also less dollars to invest and therefore reduced income from investments.

ADDITIONAL REVENURE ISSUES

Beyond the sources of revenue already discussed, an understanding of other issues which affect revenues is helpful. Below are several questions and answers which will clarify other important revenue issues.

- How does the Illinois lottery affect K-12 public school funding?

Almost everyone has heard that the primary argument posed by original lottery proponents was that lottery revenues would benefit public education, right? Well, the truth is that lottery revenues do fund public education and have certainly increased school funding; however, they have not had the impact most citizens expected.

This is a how the process works. Lottery revenues are collected by the state. After paying for prizes and expenses, the profit is placed in the Common School Fund. However, instead of earmarking all lottery funds as new revenue to fund public education, some are used to supplant present funding sources. Political leaders can, if they so choose, say that all lottery dollars went to public education but avoid pointing out that simultaneously other education funding was reduced (Illinois School Board Association, 2006).

- Why is Illinois allowed to operate with large funding inequities among school districts when other states such as Texas have had their school funding systems declared unconstitutional?

On the surface, this would seem unfair. Yet the reason is quite simple. The Illinois Constitution only states that equitable funding is a goal not a requirement (White, 2007). As a result, no legal basis exists to declare our system unconstitutional. Without a change in the State Constitution, the focus of school funding will likely remain on finding ways to address inequities through the legislative versus judicial process.

- What is a TIF district and how does it affect school district revenues?

A Tax Increment Financing district, TIF, is tool created through state legislation, which allows municipalities which otherwise would not have adequate resources a vehicle to provide the financial assistance necessary to redevelop blighted areas. In essence, one taxing body, the municipality, is allowed to divert future property tax dollars from another taxing body, a school district, to pay for improvements (Benson, 2006). Common TIF projects include redevelopment of commercial and industrial sites, renovation of existing residential and commercial building, acquisition of land, and infrastructure improvements (Illinois TIF, 2012).

According to The Illinois Tax Increment Association, under a TIF, the value of the property at the time the TIF is established serves as a baseline. Taxing bodies such as school districts continue to receive property taxes calculated on this "base" or fixed value at the beginning of the TIF for its duration. However, as the property increases in value, the additional taxes generated beyond the "base" are used by the municipality to pay for TIF improvements. The difference between the "base" value of the property and the future increased value is what is referred to as the increment (The Illinois Tax Increment Financing Association, 2012).

At the end of the TIF, which is usually 23 years but can be either shorter or longer depending upon need and legal requirements, all taxing bodies ultimately receive the new property value. In almost all instances, the new value is considerably higher since significant improvements were made to the blighted property (The Illinois Tax Increment Financing Association, 2012).

School districts are generally negatively affected by a TIF because the value of the property for tax purposes is frozen for many years. Even though ultimately a TIF will likely generate increased property tax revenues, the loss of increases in property tax revenue during the life of the TIF district means less school district revenue.

School administrators working with their boards of education may challenge the validity of a TIF or attempt to negotiate a compromise in the distribution of increased taxes generated during the TIF. At times, this can be an uphill battle. Sometimes this process creates animosity between the two units of government whose interests may be at odds. However, some districts have succeeded in convincing their municipalities to return a portion of TIF funds to their school districts annually. You can increase your chances for some financial consideration if you are cooperative rather than confrontational. It is more effective to work cooperatively with the municipality. At the same time, it is also important to monitor TIF's regularly. Do not assume that your needs will never be considered.

- If you make the assumption that you have two identical homes with all other property tax-related factors held constant across the street from each other, one in Cook County and the other in Lake, why would the Cook homeowner pay less property tax?

Although this scenario as presented is unrealistic, it does demonstrate why Cook County residential taxpayers generally have lower property taxes on properties then those

in other counties with similar EAVs. At first look, you might guess that the property taxes are lower because Cook has substantially more business property. However, the actual reason is that Cook County residential properties are assessed by law at 10% while businesses are assessed at a much higher assessment level (25%). This means that businesses pay a larger percentage of taxes than homeowners. Since residential and business property owners in all other counties are assessed rate at 33%, homeowners theoretically pay the same proportion of property taxes to the school district as businesses.

- What is a tax exempt school district educational foundation?

In recent years as school districts searched for additional sources of revenue, some have considered establishing educational foundations. In concept, a foundation must be organized as a not-for-profit organization. School district foundations are typically overseen by an independent board that accepts donations and gifts. The foundation board distributes funds as it chooses (Braun, 2010).

Highly successful school district foundations are more the exception than the rule and more prevalent in affluent school districts. Many start with great enthusiasm but fail due to unsustainable interest and/or lack of substantial funding. These foundations often target specific projects or use funds to encourage innovation. As such, they supplement the current program rather than reduce budget deficits.

There are, though, exceptions. A few Illinois school district have well functioning and ongoing foundations, which annually raise substantial revenue. The Winnetka Schools Foundation regularly raises at least $300,000 which is used to fund such programs as teacher mini-grants, sports and club programs, and more (Mesic, 2007).

SUMMARY

In Chapter 3, we have examined the primary sources of school district revenues. Furthermore, we studied the two largest revenue sources: the Illinois property tax and state aid. We also discussed the role politics plays in school governance and funding and additional revenue issues which further impact school district revenues.

Finally, as you have probably surmised, school districts have limited revenue sources. What is equally disconcerting is that school districts have very little influence over the amount of revenue most of these can generate, and for those over which it does have some control such as competitive grants and local fees, the amounts often represent a very small proportion of overall district revenues.

Chapter 4

Expenditures

In Chapter 3, we examined the primary sources of revenue to understand where school districts find the dollars to operate. In this chapter, we will focus our attention on the other side of the equation, expenditures; that is, school district spending. A good starting point for our discussion is to understand the definition of a school district budget as well as the unique accounting structure, fund accounting, under which Illinois public schools function.

SCHOOL DISTRICT BUDGET

What exactly is a school district budget? In its most basic form, a budget is a school district spending plan approved by the local board of education that allows the district administration the authority to spend district funds. Since only the board of education has legal authority to expend district funds, all expenditures must be approved by the board.

FUND ACCOUNTING

In Illinois, school districts are required by law to report school spending through a fund accounting process (Braun, 2010). Fund accounting is very different from that used in the business world and therefore sometimes appears foreign to new school board members and residents.

Under this accounting structure, a school district's budget is divided into several individual funds to which certain revenues are assigned and expenditures deducted. A good way to conceptualize fund accounting is to think of each fund as a separate checkbook established for specific expenses. For example, teacher salaries can be paid from the Education but not the Transportation Fund.

School district budgets are composed of several specific funds which are somewhat expenditure specific and governed by state regulations including transfer restrictions (Braun, 2010). By requiring that certain expenditures be paid from specific funds, Illinois helps ensure that school districts do not, for example, postpone important maintenance projects to fund teachers' salaries. The Illinois State Board of Education defines each of these funds in its 23 Illinois Administrative Code 100.Table A. What is most important for you to understand are not the plethora of requirements associated with fund accounting but rather the structure and basic characteristics of each fund.

BUDGET FUNDS

Education Funds

The Education Fund is by far the largest and most versatile of all funds and is used for the bulk of school district expenditures including educational expenses such as salaries and benefits related to the instructional program, administration, educational materials, staff development, childcare programming, special education, and the lunch program. The Education Fund also includes a sub-fund for Special Education. In fact, any district expense not specifically included in another fund can be paid from the Education Fund.

Operation and Maintenance

Expenses related to the operation and maintenance of facilities including employee salaries, benefits, contractual maintenance, supplies, utilities, and capital improvement projects are included in this fund. Revenues for the Operations and Maintenance Fund come from property taxes, building rental, and interest income.

Transportation

As the name indicates, this fund focuses on transportation expenses. The Transportation Fund receives revenues from property taxes, student fees, and state transportation aid, which are used for such expenditures as driver salaries and benefits, contract bus service costs, gasoline, maintenance, and transportation-related insurances.

Illinois Municipal Retirement and Social Security

Non-certified employees such as teacher assistants or custodians who work a minimum of 600 hours a year participate in a pension plan called the Illinois Municipal Retirement Fund (Illinois Municipal Retirement Fund, 2012). The school board collects property taxes and also utilizes CPPRT and interest to make payments on behalf of eligible employees to IMRF. This fund also pays the board share of social security and Medicare. This fund is supported primarily by property taxes.

Debt Service

The Debt Service Fund (formerly the Bond and Interest Fund) uses tax revenues to pay the principal and interest on bonds and service charges on other long-term debt instruments. Long-term is defined as a minimum of thirteen months. This fund also is used for payment of capital leases for such items as copiers, using funds transferred from the Education Fund.

Capital Projects

This fund is used to pay for major facility related capital improvements. Revenues for this fund can come from property taxes or building bond proceeds.

Fire Prevention and Safety

This fund is limited to paying expenses for capital improvements approved by the State of Illinois as life-safety projects. Revenues for this fund can come from property taxes or life-safety bond proceeds.

Working Cash

For all practical purposes, the Working Cash Fund is a cash flow account that a school district can tap as needs dictate. The Working Cash Fund can accept property tax receipts or proceeds from the sale of certain school bonds; however, no expenditures can be made from it. Rather, this fund can lend dollars as needed to other funds. Some or all of the fund's reserves may be permanently transferred to another fund. Specific laws govern these types of transaction

Tort Immunity and Judgment

The Tort and Immunity and Judgment Fund is used to pay the cost of district insurance and risk management as well as payments or tort judgments. It is funded through tax levies and/or bonds.

EXPENDITURES

Under fund accounting, school district expenditures within each fund are categorized in two ways: purpose and type. First, expenditures are designated by their purpose or "function":

- Instruction
- Support Services
- Community Services
- Debt Service
- Payment to Other Districts and Governmental Units

Within each of the above categories, expenditures are further assigned to a specific subcategory. For example, in the Education Fund, instruction expenditures are defined as one of ten sub-purposes:

- Regular Programs
- Special Education Programs
- Adult/Continuing Education
- Vocational Programs
- Interscholastic Programs
- Summer School Programs
- Gifted Programs
- Bilingual Programs
- Truant Alternative &Optional Programs

In addition to being categorized by purpose, Expenditures must also be identified by type or "object". As a result, each is assigned to one of the following:

- Salaries
- Employee Benefits
- Purchased Services
- Supplies &Materials
- Capital Outlay
- Other Objects
- Non-Capitalized Equipment
- Termination Benefits

To illustrate this process, let's consider how the cost of board-paid teacher dental insurance would be designated. First, it would be charged to the Education Fund since it is an educational expense. It would be further categorized under Instruction as Regular Programs and an Employee Benefit.

This accounting code system was created to achieve some comparability and accountability in reporting among Illinois school districts. Under this system, the Illinois State Board of Education is able to generate a variety of reports of which the most recognizable is the Illinois State School Report Card, an accountability document aimed at the public.

Definitions of Type-categories

Although some of the sub-categories such as salaries and employee benefits are self-explanatory, the others require some definition. Please find below examples of the most common categories of expenditures found under these.

Expenditures

Purchased Services

- Consultants
- Legal fees
- Copier maintenance
- Contract services such as the lunch program
- Building services such as heating, ventilation, and air conditioning maintenance

Supplies and Materials

- Instructional materials
- Office supplies, cleaning products
- Utility costs
- Food products

Capital Outlay (Durable items usually over $2000 designed to be used for multiple years)

- Computers
- Busses
- Construction projects

Other Objects

- Membership dues
- Bond payments
- Tuition for special education students
- Transfers

Non-Capitalized Equipment

- Durable items between $500 - $2000

Termination Benefits

- Payments to terminated or retiring employees as compensation for unused sick and vacation days

BUDGET REQUIREMENTS

Annual Financial Reports

Besides ensuring continuity of school district financial reporting, the prescribed fund accounting procedures are essential to the completion of various state reports. Discussed below are several reports which must either be completed by the school district or generated by the Illinois State Board of Education based on school-district supplied data. School districts are required to submit their budgets after local school board approval to the ISBE by the end of September. Since it is a budget, this is the school district spending plan for the year.

After the end of the fiscal year, school districts submit a report entitled the Annual Financial Report (AFR), which documents the actual spending of district funds. The district's revenues and expenditures are verified as part of the mandated annual audit conducted by an independent outside municipal accounting firm. Both of these are prepared under the ISBE-mandated fund accounting structure.

Annual School District Audit

School districts are required to have their financial records audited annually by an independent auditor approved the board of education. The primary purpose of an audit is to examine the school district's financial records to determine if they fairly represent the school district's financial position. The audit also provides a review of the school district's internal bookkeeping procedures and controls.

Deficit Reduction Plan

School districts that operate under an overall deficit budget must complete a mandated Deficit Reduction Plan in which they explain how they plan to eliminate their deficit (Braun, 2010). This process emerged after a school district reached a severe financial crisis stage and the state legislature determined that the school district financial monitoring process was not adequate. For this report, the definition of deficit is different from that used in our earlier discussion of an annual district deficit.

When we discussed local school district deficits in Chapter 1, a budget deficit was defined as any yearly budget in which expenditures were exceeded revenues. Districts, though, even with annual budget deficits, usually have sufficient reserves to offset anticipated shortfalls. Under the Deficit Reduction Plan, these districts would not be required to submit a plan. Only those school districts which did not have projected reserves to offset the projected deficit must develop a budget reduction plan. Since most districts, even those with annual budget deficit generally have some reserves, only those in the most financial difficulty would be required to do so.

Administrative Cost Cap

Since FY99, school districts have been required to limit administrative expenditure increases to 5%. School district administrators must ensure that designated budget line items related to administrative costs do not exceed this limit when submitting their school district's annual budget and Annual Financial Report to ISBE (Braun, 2010).

Fiduciary Responsibility

School district employees and school board members have an important ethical and moral obligation to manage and account for school district funds, especially for the benefit of students. This is called their fiduciary responsibility.

SCHOOL DISTRICT FINANCIAL PROFILE

Annually, all Illinois school districts receive a School District Rating from the Illinois State Board of Education. Its primary purpose is to analyze and monitor the finances of school districts (Illinois State Board of Education, 2012d).

The Illinois State Board of Education utilizes five financial indicators in arriving at a district's designation.

- Fund balance to revenue ratio
- Expenditure to revenue ratio
- Days cash on hand
- Percent of short-term borrowing ability remaining
- Percentage of long-term debt margin remaining

Using a quantitative score and weighting system for the indicator, school districts are assigned to one of four categories:

- Financial Recognition
- Financial Review
- Financial Early Warning
- Financial Watch

For most school districts, the School District Financial Profile has relatively little significance. Its greatest impact is primarily political. For example, it is not uncommon for a school district to be rated in the Financial Recognition category because at the moment it has a overall reserve but at the same time is trending toward financial difficulty due to a growing school budget deficit. The high rating may be a stumbling block for school districts that hope to pass an operating fund referendum now rather than wait until the district is approaching crisis. More specific information on the Illinois

School District Financial Profile system is available on the Illinois State Board of Education website (http://www.isbe.state.il.us) under School Business Services.

BUDGETING METHODS

School districts use various methods to establish the actual budget amount in line items particularly at the school level. Costs for such items as salaries and benefits are generally linked to staffing levels, negotiated contracts, insurance premiums, and local board policies and therefore are calculated based on these factors. However, for school-level budget items for which the administration has substantial control such as instructional materials, supplies, and capital expenditures, district level administrators often approach the budgeting process from different perspectives. The two most common budget allocations approaches are fixed allocation and zero-based budgeting.

Fixed Allocation

A popular approach employed by school district central office administrators to allocate funds for district programs and individual school is the fixed allocation method. Through this approach, usually a fixed percentage often tied to the rate of inflation is allocated to each district program area and individual schools. For example, a building principal may receive a set percentage increase for all grade levels and subject areas for instructional materials and supplies. Through this method, each grade level, subject area, or other building-level program receives a fixed percentage increase.

However, it is common under this approach for the superintendent to allow principals the discretion to adjust the distribution of the overall allocation between line items as deemed necessary. However, the overall amount allocated to the school is fixed at a certain percentage or dollar amount. Also, in instances where enrollment fluctuations occur, special programs are implemented, or unique capital needs exist, additional dollars may be allocated beyond the fixed amount.

Zero-Based Budgeting

This approach to budget allocation, which emerged in the 1970s, was called zero-based budgeting. Although it is less prevalent today, nonetheless, some school districts use this approach or some variance of it to set allocation levels. The concept behind the zero-based budgeting model is that funds should only be allocated based on actual needs, and thereby reduce unnecessary spending. Under zero-based budgeting, funds are allocated based on projected needs rather than prior year's funding levels. For example, school principals would be required to "make a case" for all budget fund requests. Through this process, they would need to justify program needs before actual budgeted amounts would be established.

It is, though, often criticized as too time consuming or unnecessary since allocations are often too small to justify the additional work entailed to implement. The use of a full zero-based budget model is not common; however, it is not usual for school districts to employ elements of the model as part of a fixed allocation process.

STUDENT ACTIVITY FUND

In addition to the regular budget accounts, school districts maintain activity fund accounts. These are typically used to manage funds from student-related clubs and activities. However, a school board may choose to include funds from parent and employee groups (Boer, 2004). A common example is a school's Social Fund. Teachers collect dollars from staff members, which are used to purchase gifts for events such as births, weddings, illness, and retirements.

Although these accounts are separate from those of the district, school boards have a fiduciary responsibility under the Illinois School Code, Section 10-20.19(3), to manage all funds properly even though activity fund accounts are not district funds. As such, school boards must establish policies and administrative procedures to meet their fiduciary responsibility. It is important to note that activity funds are audited during the annual school district audit (Boer, 2004).

Even though school boards have the legal responsibility for activity fund accounts, day-to-day management rests with the administration. As a result, administrators must be especially vigilant managing all aspects of the activity fund process. This is especially important since activity fund revenues are often cash-based and handled by parents, teachers, and support personnel (Boer, 2004).

SUMMARY

The focus of this chapter was the expenditure side of the equation. After discussing what constitutes a school district budget, we examined Illinois fund accounting requirements. We also studied budget requirements, the state School District Financial Profile system, and common approaches school districts employ to determine program and building-level budget allocations.

Chapter 5

Tax Caps

One of the most often misunderstood pieces of Illinois school finance legislation is the Property Tax Extension Limitation Law (PTELL) or as it is usually called – the property tax cap, which was created to slow the escalating growth of property taxes.

PTELL initially included only the collar counties of Chicago (DuPage, Kane, Lake, McHenry, and Will) when it was passed in 1991 was subsequently extended to Cook in 1994. Ultimately, all Illinois counties were given the option to extend PTELL to property in their counties although not all chose to do so. (Illinois Department of Revenue, 2012). The figure above shows the latest status of the tax cap in Illinois counties (Illinois Association of School Administrators, 2012).

TAX CAP PROVISIONS

In order to slow the growth of property taxes, legislators focused the tax cap on the governmental units' property tax extensions, the amount of property taxes the school district received the prior year. Therefore, under PTELL, a school district's property tax extension can increase annually up to 5% or the rate of inflation as measured by the All-Urban Consumer Price Index (CPI), which ever is less. Since 1990, the CPI has not exceeded 5%. The history of the PTELL limit (Illinois Department of Revenue, 2012) is shown in the table below.

Table 5.1
History of CPI

Year	December CPI-U	% CPI Increase from Prior Year	% PTELL Limit	Levy Year	Year Taxes Paid
1989	126.1				
1990	133.8	6.1	5.0	1991	1993
1991	137.9	3.1	3.1	1992	1993
1992	141.1	2.9	2.9	1993	1994
1993	145.8	2.7	2.7 (5% for Cook)	1994	1995
1994	149.7	2.7	2.7	1995	1996
1995	153.5	2.5	2.5	1996	1997
1996	158.6	3.3	3.3	1997	1998
1997	161.3	1.7	1.7	1998	1999
1998	163.9	1.6	1.6	1999	2000
1999	168.3	2.7	2.7	2000	2001
2000	174.0	3.4	3.4	2001	2002
2001	176.7	1.6	1.6	2002	2003
2002	180.9	2.4	2.4	2003	2004
2003	184.3	1.9	1.9	2004	2005
2004	190.3	3.3	3.3	2005	2006
2005	196.8	3.4	3.4	2006	2007
2006	201.8	2.5	2.5	2007	2008
2007	210.036	4.08	4.1	2008	2009
2008	210.228	0.1	0.1	2009	2010
2009	215.949	2.7	2.7	2010	2011
2010	219.179	1.5	1.5	2011	2012
2011	225.672	3.0	3.0	2012	2013

To illustrate how the tax cap works, let's consider an example. If a school district has a property tax extension of $20,000,000 in tax year 2011 and the tax cap for the next year was 3.0%, this means that the school district is only entitled to collect 3.0% more or $20,600,000 for tax year 2012.

Limiting property tax revenues to the CPI or 5% can be especially onerous to growing school districts. Therefore, when PTELL became law, a provision was included which allows school districts to receive increased property taxes beyond the 5% or CPI level for something called "new growth."

Without some provision for additional revenues with increasing enrollment, this could be a real problem for school districts. For example, what would a school district do if it experienced a substantial increase in enrollment because of a new townhouse development but could only increase its property tax revenue by 3%? Fortunately, legislators recognized this issue when they designed PTELL.

NEW GROWTH PROVISION

Since communities are constantly evolving, legislators recognized that some provision was needed to adjust for changes such as enrollment growth. The provision, commonly referred to as "new growth," allows school districts to levy additional property taxes for increases in the assessed value related to new construction and other improvements (Illinois Department of Revenue, 2012).

Consider this typical example. Your school district has a large parcel of vacant land. A developer receives approval to build a subdivision, which increases the enrollment of the local school district by 200 students. If it costs $8,000 to educate each student, where would you find $1,600,000 to pay for these children's education, particularly if your property tax extension was limited to 3%?

Under the new growth provision of PTELL, the school district can capture the additional property tax revenue generated by the new property which is exempt from the tax cap for the first year. This means that new property including residences and business property such as office building, shopping centers, and industrial facilities will generate additional property tax revenues beyond the cap (Kersten, 2008). The property taxes resulting from new growth may or may not be sufficient to pay the costs incurred for the additional children in this instance, but are nonetheless important. However, the school district must levy for it the first year it comes onto the tax roles or permanently loose taxes that otherwise would be attributable to the new growth.

CALCULATING NEW GROWTH

To illustrate how the new growth provision increases revenues, let's consider an example below. For illustration purposes, we will assume that the school district had a property tax extension for FY2010 of $20,000,000. The CPI (tax cap rate) for the next year is 3.0%. As we discussed earlier, under PTELL, the school district can only receive $20,600,000 in property taxes for the coming year (an increase of 3.0% over the prior year) even if actual property values increased more than the 3.0%.

However, during the year, a new hotel was placed on the tax roles. After completing the tax assessment process, the tax extension office calculated that hotel would generate another $200,000 in additional property taxes based on the district's tax rate. Because of the new growth provision, the school district was eligible to receive both the $20,600,000 plus the additional $200,000. As a result, the new extension base for the following year would be $20,800,000. As you can see, this provision is very important to tax capped school districts especially in property poor school districts, which most need every possible tax dollar available.

Table 5.2
Extension with New Growth

2010 Tax Extension	$20,000,000
2010 CPI (3.0%)	X 1.03
Maximum Collectable Taxes	$20,600,000
Hotel Property Tax Revenue	+ 200,000
New Extension Base	$20,800,000

HOME IPROVEMENT EXEMPTION

Not all new growth is immediately available to taxing bodies. Under Illinois law, the first $25,000 of EAV on new residential property is tax deferred for four years (Illinois Department of Revenue, 2012). After the fourth year, though, the $25,000 is included in the new growth figure for the following year. If a residential improvement exceeds the $25,000 figure, the amount over the exclusion is treated as new growth immediately (Kersten, 2008).

What is especially important to understand is that school districts make their property tax levy requests in December, months before assessments are finalized and the new growth figure is calculated. Since school districts do not know the amount of new growth, they must make their best guess on what amount to levy the prior December. As a result, school administrators often advise school boards to "balloon" levy, that is, ask for more property taxes than they think they are likely to receive, so that when the property tax extension is ultimately finalized, the district receives every property tax dollar permitted under PTELL, including the amount that results from new growth.

COMMON MISCONCEPTION

The most frequent misconception about the tax cap is that it caps individual property owners' tax bills. It does not. What it actually does is slow their rate of growth. PTELL caps the district's property tax extension (amount of property taxes the school districts is entitled to receive), which actually caps the revenue growth.

To understand this difference, let's consider how an individual's residential property tax is determined (See table below). The process begins with the county tax extension office calculating the total amount of Equalized Assessed Valuation (EAV) within the boundaries of the school district. For our sample school district, the total EAV is $500,000,000. In our scenario, the individual homeowner has an EAV of $50,000. This means that the homeowner's EAV is 0.0001% of the total district EAV. Therefore, the individual property owners would pay 0.0001% of the amount of property taxes due the school district. If the school district's property tax extension was $20,000,000, the homeowner would receive a bill for $2,000 or 0.0001 of $20,000,000.

Table 5.3
Proportion of EAV Calculation

Total District EAV	$500,000,000
Homeowner's EAV	$50,000
Homeowner's EAV Portion of Total EAV	0.0001
Total School District Property Tax Revenue	$20,000,000
Homeowner's Property Tax Bill	$2,000
Tax Calculation	$20,000,000 X 0.0001 = $2,000

However, some property owners could actually pay higher taxes if their proportion of the overall EAV goes up faster than someone else's (See table below). For example, if you added a home addition or made some other improvement, which increased your EAV, you would own a higher proportion of the overall EAV. Therefore, when the county extension office calculates your property tax bill, because your portion of the overall EAV is larger due to the building addition, you would pay more property taxes.

In our example, if we assume that the overall EAV remained at $500,000,000 and the homeowner's EAV increased to $65,000, the individual now has a higher percent of overall EAV (0.00013) and will pay a higher percentage of the overall property tax requested by the school district or $2,600.

Table 5.4
Proportion of EAV with Homeowner Addition

Total School District EAV	$500,000,000
Homeowner's EAV	$65,000
Homeowner's EAV Portion of Total EAV	0.00013
Total School District Property Tax Revenue	$20,000,000
Homeowner's Property Tax Bill	$2,600
Tax Calculation	$20,000,000 X 0.00013 = $2,600

Homeowners could also see their property tax bills increase due to a decrease in the overall EAV. The most common reasons that the overall EAV would decrease are either a reduction of EAV due to a business property tax appeal or a decrease in the multiplier. In Cook County where unlike other counties, the multiplier is more than 1.0 traditionally and tends to vary from year to year.

If the overall EAV goes down but a homeowner's EAV remains the same, the property owner has a higher percentage of the overall EAV. The table below provides an example of this scenario.

Table 5.5
Effect of lower Overall EAV

Total School District EAV	$480,000,000
Homeowner's EAV	$50,000
Homeowner's EAV Portion of Total EAV	0.0001041
Total District Property Tax Revenue	$20,000,000
Homeowner's Property Tax Bill	$2,083
Tax Calculation	$20,000,000 X 0.0001041 = $2,083

The opposite is also true. If, for example, the county re-assesses all property in the area and raises other property owners' assessments faster than yours, you now have a smaller proportion of the overall EAV and may be taxed less.

Although the actual property tax increase or decrease in this instance would be small, it does demonstrate how the concept of ownership of a proportion of EAV affects an individual's property tax bill.

TAX CAP REFERENDUM OPTIONS

Since the passage of PTELL, tax capped school districts are limited to specific options when requesting an operating rate increase. These are discussed in more detail in Chapter 9.

BUSINESS PROPERTY TAX APPEALS

Other factors can also affect a taxpayer's proportion of overall property taxes. The most significant are business property tax appeals. You have probably heard that large businesses regularly appeal their property tax assessments. Many negotiate lower assessment levels through the county assessor or take their case to the Board of Review before the extension is set. Property owners who choose to challenge their assessments may further appeal to the county Property Tax Appeals Board (PTAB) or the circuit court (Illinois Department of Revenue, 2012). Some, of course, study their assessments and realize that they are not likely to win a reduction.

What the public does not understand is that under the tax cap, when a business receives a tax assessment reduction, this translates into a tax increase for other taxpayers, including many residential property owners. This is because a reduction in a business' property assessment means that the business now owns a smaller proportion of the overall EAV. Other property owners now have higher proportions of the overall EAV and must pay a greater percentage of property taxes.

EFFECT OF TAX CAP

From any school district's perspective, the property tax cap law is detrimental because it substantially limits school district revenues. Other sources of revenue such as state aid do not offset the limiting effects of PTELL. The reality is that school districts must operate with their major source of revenue, property taxes, artificially capped while their costs often increase faster than the rate of inflation and are uncapped.

Consider the following questions to appreciate this point.

- How much did your healthcare premiums increase last year?
- Have your utility costs risen faster than inflation?
- How much has a gallon gasoline increased in recent years?
- What has happen to the cost of a jar of peanut butter in the past year?
- Have teacher salaries increased more than the rate of inflation?

These questions illustrate how difficult it is to manage a school district under the tax cap, particularly if you hope to maintain current levels of programs and services, when revenues are restricted and expenditures are not. This is probably the most significant factor contributing to school district deficit spending and financial stress in Illinois.

TAX CAP AND POLITICS

When was the last time you heard an Illinois politician say, "Let's raise property taxes" or "Let's eliminate PTELL" when presenting their campaign platform? We all know that it is popular to be anti-tax. As educational stakeholders, we understand the realities of school funding and cannot understand why our political leaders do not. We need to recognize that one of a politician's goals is re-election. With this goal in mind, politicians tend to be particularly sensitive to all aspects of the political process, especially constituent views. As a result, it is wise to anticipate that politicians will typically act in a political manner. If taxpayers believe that property taxes are too high and that the tax cap is a plus, you can be assured that the cap will not be repealed.

Similarly, at the district level, a substantial percentage of local residents have no direct vested interest in schools. Some never had or no longer have children in schools while others are on fixed or low incomes. These groups have little incentive to increase property taxes. School board members and administrators must recognize these realities and be prepared to respond whether at school budget and tax levy hearings or during school board elections and school referendum campaigns.

MONITORING LEGISLATION

Recently, Illinois legislators have proposed limiting the cost of living (Consumer Price Index - CPI) increases provided under PTELL for school district that have overall EAV decreases from the prior year. Such legislation would further erode limited school district revenues at a time when vendors' costs remain unrestricted. Although this legislation has not yet garnered sufficient legislator support, it continues to be a topic of legislative discussion.

SUMMARY

In Chapter 5, we have explored the legal requirements of the Illinois Property Tax Extension Limitation Law in order to understand how the tax cap impacts public school funding at the district level. In particular, we examined how it limits school district property tax revenues and learned that its main purpose is to slow the rate property owners' tax increases rather than set an actual cap on an individual's property tax. We also considered the impact of PTELL's new growth provision as well as political issues which all educational stakeholders must consider in the tax cap era.

School administrators, school board members, and other public education proponents, should closely monitor all legislative initiatives. Because school funding is at the forefront of everyone's political agendas, those with a vested interest in public education must become informed advocates for schools. They must help legislators understand the pragmatic implications of any potential legislation.

Chapter 6

Borrowing

This chapter will focus on additional options to fund school district operations: short and long-term borrowing and capital leasing. Part of the long-term borrowing discussion will explore the impact of the property tax cap law (PTELL) on the ability of school districts to issue bonds.

SHORT-TERM BORROWING

The most widely used form of short-term borrowing is the tax anticipation warrant (TAW). They are analogous to personal payday loans which individuals receive and must pay back from their next paychecks. As the name implies, a school board borrows money from a financial institution and agrees to pay back the loan with interest from taxes it anticipates receiving in the near future. In fact, by law TAWs must be paid back on a set date after the property tax receipts arrive. A school board may borrow up to 85% of the property taxes it has levied in the fund for which the warrant is issued but bonds must be repaid within 13 months (Braun, 2010).

The primary purpose of TAWs is for cash flow needs. Typically, a school district will sell tax anticipation warrants when it does not have sufficient funds available in its reserves to make payments due to employees or vendors. To some degree, TAWs are similar to credit card debt. If, for example, you need to repair your car and do not have money on hand but will soon, you may charge the repair on your credit card and pay it when the bill comes due.

Yet, similar to a person who has very little savings and has difficulty meeting unexpected expenditures, school districts that use TAWs tend to be the poorer districts with larger budget deficits and small reserves. TAWs also are an indication of financial weakness.

To illustrate this further, let's consider a recent example of events which forced some school districts to sell TAWs. As the 2007-08 school year was fast approaching, the Illinois governor and legislature were unable to meet the regular deadline for a state budget. As the state budget process continued to unfold slowly into the fall, an extension of the 7% property assessment cap for Cook County became a sticking point in a struggle of wills between the governor and other legislative leaders. Without an agreement on the 7% cap, tax bills could not be issued to Cook County property owners and consequently, no property tax revenues could be collected for school districts. As the political wrangling continued, school districts were forced to dip into their reserves to pay salaries and other costs. For those school districts that had reserves, the primary negative effect was the loss of interest on the property taxes received late. For the least wealthy districts, they not only lost interest revenue but also had to borrow money through tax anticipation warrants then pay interest on the loans too! Again, the poorest districts were impacted the most.

In addition to TAWs, you should be aware that several other short-term borrowing options exist that employed less regularly than TAWs. Unless you are in business management, you do not need to understand the specific differences. However, you should at least recognize that other options are available. If you find yourself in a situation where additional financial counsel is needed, you would most likely seek advance from specialists. Other short-term options include:

- Tax anticipation notes;
- General obligation tax anticipation warrants;
- Corporate personal property replacement tax notes;
- Revenue anticipation notes; and,
- Teachers' orders.

LONG-TERM BORROWING

Another potential source of revenues which school boards may to want consider is classified as long-term borrowing. Several distinct borrowing types are available to many school districts, each with its own unique requirements. However, before examining each of these individually, it is important to understand both the concept and legal requirements of school district debt service extension base (Illinois Department of Revenue, 2012). The extension is the amount of property taxes received the prior year.

Debt Service Extension Base

In Illinois school finance and politics, sometimes it is better to be lucky than good. So is the case with the debt extension limit. When the tax cap became law, a provision was included which established a permanent debt extension limit for school districts. The debt service extension base, which represented the existing school district debt, was based on the actual dollar amount of the tax extension in a school district's Bond and Interest Fund the year following passage of PTELL.

As you can imagine, the amount of the limit was extremely variant since it was not tied to the financial position of the district or any logical factors such as need, but merely the tax extension amount at a particular point in time. Those districts which happen to be lucky enough to have a large extension were winners while those which had no Bond and Interest levy that year were losers.

Let's examine how the debt service extension base actually works. If your school district was fortunate enough to have outstanding non-referendum bonds with a repayment in 1994 of $2,000,000, you now have a permanent $2M debt service extension base. This means that you can tax property owners up to $2M each year to pay the principal and interest on outstanding bonds. In other words, the school district may sell bonds whose payment schedule equals $2M each year including principal and interest.

What makes this a source of additional revenue is that you are able to tax the public in addition to the tax cap amount. If you were unfortunate and had no existing debt, the only way to sell bonds is to go to referendum.

Beginning with the 2009 tax levy, school district debt service extension base will increase annually by the lesser of 5% or the CPI from the prior calendar year. This new provision is important for these school districts because school boards have the potential to generate additional revenues due to the increases in the amount of bonds they are permitted to repay. Since they can tax the property owners more, they can also increase the amount they borrow.

Bonds

What exactly is a bond? In its most basic form, a bond is a loan often in $5,000 amounts that the school district makes and agrees to pay back over some specified period of time much as you might an automobile loan. Bonds must be issued for a specific purpose. School boards, which meet specific legal requirements, have the authority to issue certain types of bonds.

For the purpose of illustration, we will assume that a school board has authority to sell $7,500,000 in bonds which will be repaid over four years. As such, the district will sell the bonds, generally to large financial institutions that either include them in investment portfolios or re-sell them to other investors. As a result of the sale, the school district receives $7.5M which is placed in the school district's reserves and used as needed.

The bond holders are repaid their $7.5M plus interest over the term of the bonds i.e. the next four years. To make these re-payments, the school district is allowed to add the repayment cost to its Bond and Interest Fund levy annually but cannot receive revenue beyond the debt extension limit of $2M.

Bond Sale Process

What are the basic steps a school district takes to complete a Working Cash or Funding Bond sale? Although these can vary somewhat, Elizabeth Hennessy (2007), bond consultant for William Blair and Company, explains that a regular bond sale process normally includes:

- Discussing with the school board a financial plan, issuing a Resolution of Intent to sell bonds, and scheduling a public hearing (School District);
- Publishing the resolution in a local paper (Bond Consultant);
- Preparing preliminary bond sale documents (Bond Consultant);
- Holding a meeting with bond rating company to establish the district's bond rating (School District & Bond Consultant);
- Conducting a public hearing at a regular school board meeting (School Board);

- Conducting the bond sale (Bond Consultant and Attorney); and,
- Closing the sale of bonds (School District, Bond Consultant, & Bond Attorney)

You will note from the steps above that school administrators need to understand the general process but not be experts. Rather, they employ outside consultants and legal experts to facilitate their bond sales.

TYPES OF BONDS

Now that we have discussed the debt extension limit, defined bonds, and examined the basic bond sale process, we are ready to consider five of the most common types of school district bonds: Working Cash, Life-safety, Funding, Alternate for One Cent Sales Tax, and Building Bonds.

Working Cash Bonds

A prominent type of bond is the Working Cash Bond. Proceeds from a Working Cash Bond sale are deposited in the Working Cash Fund. From there, they can be loaned or transferred as needed to other operating funds for use for capital projects or operations (Braun, 2010). If bond proceeds are loaned, they must be paid back to the Working Cash Fund when tax dollars are received.

Let's consider some examples.

- If a school district sells $7.5M in Working Cash Bonds while operating under a $1M deficit in the Education Fund, it can transfer $1M from Working Cash to cover the deficit.
- School districts may use bond proceeds for facility renovation. If, for instance, a school district needs $2M to fund a school renovation project but only has $1M available in its Operations and Maintenance Fund, it has the option to transfer the $1M needed from the Working Cash Fund.

Working Cash Fund Bond Requirements

School districts are subject to certain requirements when they initiate a Working Cash Bond sale. First, if they want to sell the bonds as federal tax free, they must show that the funds are needed to operate the district in the immediate future. If not, the district is free to sell them as taxable bonds. Some investors are particularly interested in tax free bonds and are willing to buy them at a lower interest rate, which means that the school district will pay less interest on the bonds (Braun, 2010).

Another important fact is that Working Cash Bonds are subject to a "backdoor referendum." The term makes the sale sound "sneaky" but it is not. School districts which meet legal requirements to sell these bonds must pass a motion at an open school board meeting and publish a notice of intent to sell bonds in a local newspaper 30 days before any action. The school board then must hold a public hearing before the actual bond sale. During this time period, residents may force the school board to take the bond sale to a referendum if they can obtain the signatures of 10% of the registered voters on a petition which is submitted to the school board. The school board at this point may either hold a referendum or drop the sale. Absent the petition, the Board may proceed with the sale.

Life-Safety Bonds

Back in 1958, a horrible event occurred in the Chicago-area, which led to the creation of the Life-Safety Code. This was the Our Lady of Angels fire which resulted in the deaths of many adults and children (Our Lady of Angels Fire Memorial, 2008). This event gave impetus to the State of Illinois Life-Safety Code which contains facility standards for public schools.

Every ten years, school districts are required to hire an architect who completes a life-safety audit of school district facilities. In this report, the architect identifies any areas which fail to meet life-safety requirements and therefore may qualify for funding either through life-safety bonds or the district's life-safety levy. The architect must prepare special documents called Life-Safety Amendments which are submitted to the Illinois State Board of Education that makes the final determination on whether the project qualifies for life-safety (Braun, 2010).

For larger ISBE-approved amendments, school districts with debt service extension bases may find that the bond sale approach is preferred. For example, a common Life-Safety improvement is the replacement of a school roof. Rather, than use funds from the Operations and Maintenance Fund, a school district with a debt service extension base may sell Life-Safety Bonds to pay for the repair.

Life-Safety Fund Requirements

The most significant difference between Life-Safety and Working Cash Bonds is that the district is not subject to the backdoor referendum process for the Life-Safety bonds. In fact, the school board can sell the bonds simply by taking action at an open school board meeting following a public hearing (Braun, 2010). However, remember that a district in a tax capped county without a debt extension limit cannot realistically use this bond sale option because they would have to repay the bonds from regular revenues creating a shortage of funds in other budgeted areas. Also, school districts must plan well in advance of any planned Life-Safety bond sale since approval by both the Regional Office of Education and the state can make the process quite time consuming.

Debt Certificates

School boards may issue debt certificates for capital projects. Debt certificates are paid from the general funds of the District. There is no separate bond or interest tax levy dedicated to the re-payment of debt certificates. The District annually budgets a sufficient amount to pay the principal and interest on debt certificates. These certificates are subject to the debt service extension base.

Debt certificates offer the advantage of spreading capital costs over several budget years. They also help preserve fund balances and may be a preferred alternative when interest rates are low. On the other hand, they are not an additional revenue source but do require the school district to pay interest (Hennessy, 2012).

Funding Bonds

Funding bonds, which are subject to the debt extension limit in tax capped counties, can be sold to pay for incurred district obligations (bills). Two common uses of these bonds include paying for computer hardware or buses already purchased by the school district. However, since they are subject to a backdoor referendum, you should be caution using them. If the taxpayer challenge is successful and the district does not pass a referendum, the district must still pay for these capital items. If you are considering funding bonds, it is advisable to consult a bond attorney to ensure you understand all bond sale requirements and any potential implications.

Non-Taxed Capped Counties

School districts in non-tax capped counties have a distinct advantage over those subject to PTELL. Since they are not subject to the tax cap, they generally can sell both Working Cash and Life-Safety Bonds because their debt repayment is not limited by the debt service extension base (Illinois Department of Revenue, 2012). The primary concern for these school districts is convincing their school boards to proceed with the bond sale and ensuring that any increase associated with the bond repayment does not create consternation among local taxpayers.

Alternate Bonds for One Cent Sales Tax

In counties where voters have approved through referendum a one cent sales tax for county school facilities, the school board may issue bonds to pay for improvements. Bond maturities may not exceed 40 years. These bonds are not subject to the debt service extension base or a backdoor referendum. However, a separate fund must be established to account for revenues and expenses.

Building Bonds

The final category of long-term borrowing we will consider is Building Bonds. These are the type of bonds with which you may be familiar because they require a referendum. When a school board wants to fund the construction of a major project such as a building addition or new school, it will often proceed with a referendum because it does not have sufficient reserves to fund the project.

A school board may hold a referendum during any general election except during fall elections during odd years. If the bond sale is approved by a majority of the voters, the district may proceed. Bond proceeds are used to complete the project and additional taxes are levied over a specified period of time to pay back the bond holders with interest. These bonds are not limited by the debt service extension base (Braun, 2010).

These bonds that are, in essence, tied to "brick and motor" are typically paid back over many years. Unlike Working Cash Bonds, which often fund operational costs, Building Bonds improve facilities for generations of students, some of whom may not yet be born. Consequently, it is common to extend debt repayment over many years to ensure that those who will benefit form the improvements share in the costs.

Other Available Bond Options

Although we examined the three most prevalent types of bonds: Working Cash, Life-Safety, and Building, other variations of bonds and short-term borrowing are available. According to Braun, (2010) two other rarely used bonds available include:

- Tort judgment; and,
- Insurance reserve.

For all but school business officials, an extended discussion of these is unnecessary. Most school district administrators and school boards considering a bond sale will need to seek advice from bond consultants to identify and understand their options.

Other Borrowing

One other borrowing option for school districts is capital leasing (Braun, 2010). For school districts without sufficient reserves to purchase certain capital outlay items or which prefer to extend the payment of a large purchase over more than one year, this may be a viable alternative.

The most common uses of capital leasing are for school busses, copiers, and technology hardware. A school district will enter into a contract with a leasing agent to obtain the funds necessary to purchase needed capital items immediately. As part of the agreement, the district will pay back the loan with interest over several years. This option is especially helpful to financially needy school districts.

SUMMARY

In this chapter, we examined the primary options for short and long-term borrowing. We discussed the debt service extension base, particularly as it relates to school bonds. We studied the five primary long-term bond types including their unique characteristics as well as capital leasing.

Chapter 7

Financial Planning

Now that you are armed with a basic understanding of both the revenue and expenditures sides of the school finance equation, we are ready to discuss a critical element of fiscal management: long-range financial planning. That is, how school administrators plan for the financial health of their school districts.

A good way to conceptualize the process is to relate it to your personal financial planning. Let me begin by asking you to consider several questions.

- Would you buy a new car without considering how you would pay for it?
- Would you buy a home without weighing your relative job security?
- Would you wait until you were 65 before planning for your retirement?
- Would you buy US Savings Bonds exclusively without ever considering other investment options because you had read about them in a government advertisement?
- Would you postpone saving for your children's college educations until the day they graduated from high school?

Of course you would not. In fact, I am sure you would assess your current and potential income level, evaluate your savings plan, and consider your short and long-term liabilities. You would also begin to speculate about your personal financial future including where your career may take you and what known and unknown factors might await you. As part of this process, you would also make your best guesses on what the next few years may hold; then, as time passed, factor in new information, and adjust your financial planning course. The chances are that because you are a responsible person you would not put on a pair of blinders and just hope everything will magically work out so that you would be free to sail off on a new yacht into the retirement sunset somewhere in the Caribbean free of financial worries!

Successful school district administrators similarly plan for the financial futures of their school districts. That is, they regularly engage in long-term financial planning. The fact of the matter is that a large number of children, families, school district employees, and community members depend on the wisdom, vision, and planning skills of the school district's administration. They expect that the administration will keep abreast of the latest issues, laws, trends, and practices in order to maintain quality educational programs and services, all while keeping the school district as financially solvent as possible. I use "as possible" because even under sound administrative leadership, financial crisis may be inevitable. Administrators sometimes have little or no control over some factors. Yet, for most districts, sound long-range financial planning may be the difference between successful financial problem-solving and crisis management.

LONG-RANGE FINANCIAL PLANNING

What exactly is long-range financial planning? It is a process which central office administrators use to project the long-term financial health of the school district and ultimately make decisions which affect the educational program and services offered. Through a long-range financial planning process, most administrators will look out over the next five years and make their best informed estimate of the future financial position of the school district.

Financial projections must be built on solid data and realistic assumptions to be useful. If so, they are usually quite accurate for a year or two. However, because the future is subject to change and projections are primarily forecasts of trends and/or a range of possibilities, they become increasingly imprecise after a couple of years. Even though projections are reasonably valid only for the short-term, prudent administrators know that they must plan for five years to order to ensure that they are taking into consideration as broad a perspective as possible. Otherwise, through short-sighted thinking, they may plunge the district into financial crisis in a relatively short period of time.

Consider this example. A school district has a reserve of $20M and an annual budget of $40M. At first look, you might say that the school district is very solvent. However, if you look more closely, you may find a different picture. For example, if the school district is experiencing a $3M annual budget deficit and property tax revenue is increasing only at the rate of inflation while other costs including salaries are outstripping inflation by at least 3%, or if the school board is planning to add several new programs while also reducing class size by three students, the $20M reserve will disappear within 5 years. If you had just looked at the current year, you could conclude that the district is financially stable. However, if you considered all information available, your analysis would be much different. It is precisely for this reason that school district administrators must maintain a multi-year perspective if they are to project a relatively accurate picture of the district's financial future.

PREPARING FINANCIAL PROJECTIONS

The process of preparing financial projections begins with the selection of a financial software tool. School administrators typically purchase a commercial product or develop their own which could include a regular spreadsheet. A good way to gather information to help you decide what approach to use is to network with other school business officials or superintendents in your area. They can be a valuable resource to you.

After selecting the tool, the next step is to identify revenue and expenditure assumptions. In order to develop useful projections, you must make some assumptions (informed estimates) of what will happen on the revenue and expenditure sides of the equation over the next few years. The decisions you make during this phase are critical in the projection process. In fact, the more accurate your assumptions are, the more useful your projections. On the other hand, if your assumptions are either too high or low, your projections will be essentially useless and your credibility as a financial manager will be called into question.

As a result, one of the most important responsibilities in financial planning is doing your "homework." Seasoned school business officials know that the recent past is often a good predictor of the near future. Therefore, they gather as much information as possible from the immediate past and combine it with their best estimates of future trends to develop revenue and expenditure assumptions. Typical areas to study include:

- Recent pertinent school district data such as staffing patterns, retirements, enrollment, educational program and facility needs, insurance costs, and collective bargaining agreements;
- Recent statewide data on PTELL levels, state aid support, and unfunded mandates;
- Property tax assessments including new growth and business property tax appeals;
- State and federal funding levels; and,
- Pending state and federal legislation.

In addition, administrators gather as much information as possible from federal and state agencies as well as professional organizations and private sources to thoroughly understand any factors which may impact school funding. Finally, they actively lobby legislators and other key officials who are the educational policy makers. Only through such a thorough and informed inquiry process can school administrators be well prepared to develop sound 5-year financial projections.

To illustrate common financial projection assumptions, I have included below revenue and expenditure assumptions for a sample school district. Later in this chapter, I will use these assumptions as the basis for a set of five-year projections.

- Tax revenues are projected within the constraints of the tax cap and business property tax appeals
- The tax cap is projected at 3.0%
- Equalized Assessed Valuation (EAV) of the District is projected to increase due to new property growth (based on information on new property) and reassessment increases of 10% in triennial years 2007, 2010, and 2013, and 3% in non-triennial years
- Interest revenue is projected at a 4% rate of return on invested reserves
- Interest earned on the Bond & Interest fund balance is transferred to Education Fund
- Lunch, fees and other local revenue are projected to increase 3% per year

- State Aid, CPPTRR, and federal aid are projected to remain constant at a level based on the average of the last 3 years

Sample Expenditure Assumptions

- Enrollment and staffing are projected to remain constant
- Total salary costs are projected to increase 4.0% per year
- Benefit and utility costs are expected to increase 10% per year
- Service cost increases are estimated at 7% per year
- Special education tuition costs are projected to increase 10% per year
- Expendable material and equipment cost increases are held at 5% per year

Earlier in this chapter, I noted that financial projections are relatively accurate for a couple of years. However, since projections are built on assumptions (best guesses) with a goal of showing trends and a range of possibilities, the future is often somewhat different from what is predicted. As a result, financial projections become increasing imprecise as years pass. If you had some mystical power to know the future, that would be wonderful; but you do not. What you quickly learn through the financial planning process is that you will encounter many unknowns and must regularly adjust your projections to maintain accuracy.

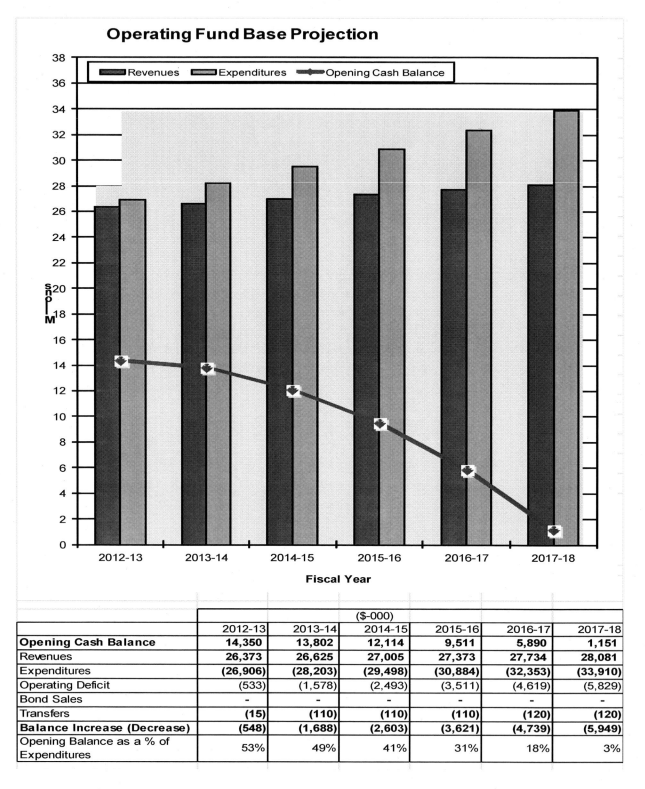

			($-000)			
	2012-13	2013-14	2014-15	2015-16	2016-17	2017-18
Opening Cash Balance	**14,350**	**13,802**	**12,114**	**9,511**	**5,890**	**1,151**
Revenues	26,373	26,625	27,005	27,373	27,734	28,081
Expenditures	(26,906)	(28,203)	(29,498)	(30,884)	(32,353)	(33,910)
Operating Deficit	(533)	(1,578)	(2,493)	(3,511)	(4,619)	(5,829)
Bond Sales	-	-	-	-	-	-
Transfers	**(15)**	**(110)**	**(110)**	**(110)**	**(120)**	**(120)**
Balance Increase (Decrease)	**(548)**	**(1,688)**	**(2,603)**	**(3,621)**	**(4,739)**	**(5,949)**
Opening Balance as a % of Expenditures	53%	49%	41%	31%	18%	3%

Figure 7.1. Five-Year Financial Projection

Before we study the figure above, please note that financial projections exclude the Bond and Interest Fund since it is outside the tax cap.

In the bar graph, the left bar (green) represents the revenues and the right (Blue) expenditures. The line shows the opening cash balance; in other words, the amount of dollars which the district had on July 1 of a particular school year.

You will note that the first year of the projections is the most recent one for which all data are known. It is from this point that school business officials apply their assumptions to project revenues and expenditures for subsequent years.

Let's begin by understanding how to read the bar graph and financial data. On the left hand side of the bar graph are numbers representing dollar levels. At the bottom are the current and projected school years. If you examine FY2013, you see that the school district had revenues (green bar) of $26,373,000 (26,373M) and expenditures (blue bar) of $26,906,000 (26,906M). The red line shows that the district began the 2012-13 school year with an opening balance of $14,350,000 ($14,350M).

Reading the chart, you also see that the district had an operating deficit that year of $533,000 because expenditures ($26,906M) exceeded revenues (($26,373M) by $533,000. The district also transferred funds to the Bond and Interest Fund, which added another $15,000 in expenditures. Overall, the district's cash balance at the end of FY13 dropped to $13,802M, the amount of the next year's opening balance.

Another way to categorize a district's financial position is to calculate the ratio of the year's opening balance as a percent of the year's expenditures. The higher the figure, the better is the district's financial position.

In Figure 7.1, you see that this school district begins FY14 with $13,802M and anticipates expenditures of $26,625M. To calculate its opening balance as a percent of expenditures, you merely divide $13,802M Opening Cash Balance by $26,625M Expenditures and see that the district begins the FY14 school year with enough reserves to pay 49.0% of the year's expenditures. For most school districts, this is an enviable position. Before they receive any revenues, they know that they have sufficient reserves to pay more than half of next year's costs.

Here, though, is where we see the real value of long-term projections. If you just looked at the large cash reserve and the 49.0% figure, you could conclude that this district has no financial concerns. However, when you begin to factor in the assumptions including the growing deficit over five years, the picture begins to change dramatically.

INTERPRETING THE PROJECTIONS

Now that you can read the projections, let's interpret them. As I approach my projections, I first take a global look at the overall financial picture of the district. Ask yourself this question. When you study the graph, is this a positive or negative financial projection? What I see is a district heading toward financial difficulty. Under the assumptions, expenditures are rising at a much faster rate than revenues as the costs of salaries, benefits, supplies, and services are projected to far exceed the inflation-based revenue increases limited by the tax cap. To understand this, study the salary and expenditure lines across the five projected year. You also note that the red line (opening balance) is dropping quickly during the projection period. If the district does not increase revenues or reduce expenditures, between FY 13 and FY18, the district's overall opening balance will have dropped by $13,199M signaling a pending financial crisis.

The value of projections is that they allow the school district administration and board of education to have time to study the district's financial future and begin to make adjustments now that will improve the long-term outlook. A good rule of thumb is to make as many adjustments as early as possible since the effect of either revenue increases or expenditure reductions is compounded over time. That is, a small change today has a much bigger impact than waiting three years.

A good analogy which may help you understand the power of compounding is to consider what financial planners tell their clients about retirement planning. They always advise people to start savings as soon as possible, preferably in their early twenties rather than waiting until they are in their 40s. They know that this strategy translates into a much higher portfolio value at retirement. In fact, you can actually invest significantly less when you are 20s than if you wait until your 40s and retire with the same or even more funds, primarily because of compounding.

WORKING WITH PROJECTIONS

Financial projections should be used as an ongoing planning tool by school administrators to monitor the financial position of the school district and to assist in decision-making. Experienced administrators typically update financial projections regularly during the year as new information becomes available and present annual projections to the board of education as part of the yearly budget development process.

Administrators can also use financial projections as a planning tool. By altering the revenue and expenditure assumptions or making changes to revenues and/or expenditures, you can test the impact of any actions you are considering prior to recommending them to the board of education.

To illustrate the use of projections as a planning tool, let's study the impact of a one time expenditure reduction coupled with a working cash bond sale can have on the basic projection above. In this scenario, the tax capped school district has an annual debt service extension base of $1.5M. This means that the district can sell $3M in bonds and repay them over two years. Under this approach, they can sell bonds every other year.

Proposed Actions

Listed below are actions that the superintendent and the school business official are considering. The question is - What would be the likely impact on the school district's five-year financial projections if these actions were taken?

Revenue Enhancement

- $3M Working Cash Bond Sale Every Two Years

Expenditure Reductions

- $300,000 - 5 teachers
- $100,000 - Teacher Assistants/Clerical Staff
- $50,000 - Benefits
- $100,000 - 5% Service Reductions
- $80,000 - 10% Supply Reductions

Financial Projections

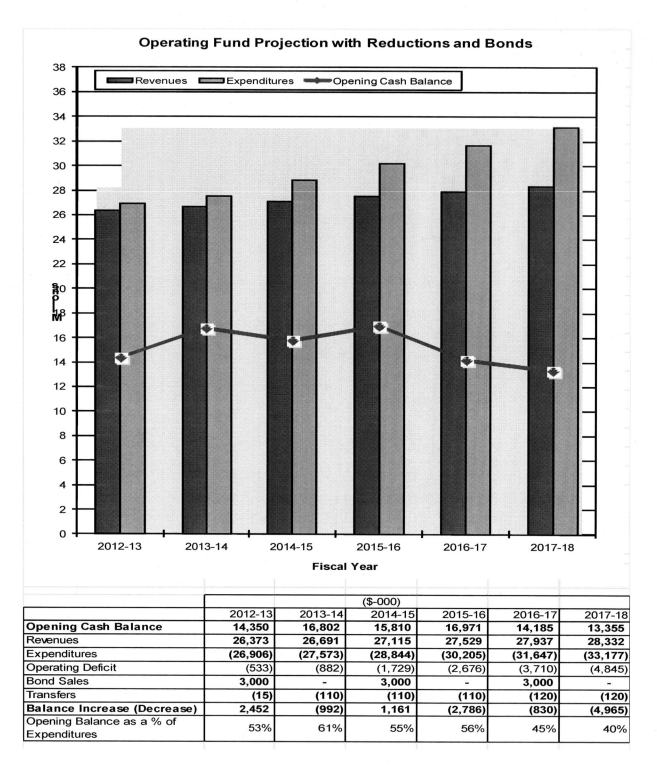

	($-000)					
	2012-13	2013-14	2014-15	2015-16	2016-17	2017-18
Opening Cash Balance	**14,350**	**16,802**	**15,810**	**16,971**	**14,185**	**13,355**
Revenues	26,373	26,691	27,115	27,529	27,937	28,332
Expenditures	(26,906)	(27,573)	(28,844)	(30,205)	(31,647)	(33,177)
Operating Deficit	(533)	(882)	(1,729)	(2,676)	(3,710)	(4,845)
Bond Sales	3,000	-	3,000	-	3,000	-
Transfers	(15)	(110)	(110)	(110)	(120)	(120)
Balance Increase (Decrease)	**2,452**	**(992)**	**1,161**	**(2,786)**	**(830)**	**(4,965)**
Opening Balance as a % of Expenditures	53%	61%	55%	56%	45%	40%

Figure 7.1. Five-Year Financial Projection with Proposed Actions

63

Impact of Proposed Changes. By implementing a one-time $630,000 expenditure reduction while selling working cash bonds every two years, the district would substantially improve it five-year financial picture. Under the original base projections, the school district would open FY18 with a balance of $1,151,000. However, by taking the proposed actions, this district would enter FY 18 with an opening cash balance of $13,355M. Although you may not be able to increase your revenues as substantially, you could propose district-specific changes and study their impact on your district's financial position.

SUMMARY

Chapter 7 explored the efficacy of financial planning in school district management. Also discussed was the financial planning process, including the development of five-year projections. Finally, we looked at the uses and limitations inherent in school district financial planning as well as the importance of planning for sound fiscal management.

Chapter 8

Personnel

School districts are people businesses. At the risk of pointing out the obvious, the single largest expense in any school district is employee-related. For most school districts, salaries account for 60% or more of all expenditures. Therefore, an important consideration for any district administrator is the cost associated with employees. In this chapter, we will examine how school districts determine staffing levels and employee compensation. We will also look at common employee benefits and retirement systems.

STAFFING PATTERNS

No one approach to staffing is pervasive in Illinois school districts. The reality is that school districts often choose staffing approaches that reflect local factors. Some districts are highly unionized, while others tend to be somewhat paternalistic. In certain instances, parents are very influential in district policy setting; while in others, community groups or teachers have a strong voice in many matters. As a result, issues related to collective bargaining or political forces associated with employee, parent, and community groups will influence how the school board staffs its schools.

Some school districts establish firm staffing ratios either through board policy or collective bargaining agreements. For example, a school board may set a policy which states that no kindergarten class may exceed 23 students; while in others, collective bargaining agreements include class size maximums. Under either approach, if any class section exceeds the cap, the school district adds a new class section.

Other school districts operate under staffing guidelines which do not automatically require the addition of a new class when a section exceeds a maximum enrollment. Rather, the guidelines, which are usually written as administrative procedures, serve as a preferred class size range. Under this model, the administration and school board retain the authority to determine final staffing levels. See a sample of staffing guidelines below (Table 8.1).

The firm staffing ratio method can be problematic for school districts, especially those with limited classroom space or financial concerns, since the addition of a new class section is mandatory. In contrast, staffing guidelines facilitate a thoughtful approach to management without the inflexibility associated with firm maximums. School districts would be well advised to maintain a flexible rather than a firm staffing ratio approach.

Not all school districts have staffing models. In these instances, no specific staffing ratio requirement or guideline exists. For some districts, this approach is effective. Staffing decisions are made by the school board on a case-by-case basis often on the counsel of the district administration or by delegation to the administration. However, the absence of a formal policy or procedures may create some internal or external issues often related to inequities.

Class size issues can become a source of conflict within school districts. It is not unusual for parents and teachers to lobby administrators and school board members, often at open board meetings, to lower class size. Also, controversies periodically emerge when special education students are mainstreamed into regular classes for parts of a school day. The issue usually centers on whether the guidelines should be altered to reflect the partial mainstreaming of special education students. Although staffing ratios or guidelines are no guarantee of political stability, they can provide a structure to help focus discussion.

Table 8.1
Sample Staffing Guidelines

Grade	Range	Maximums	Number of Sections			
			2	3	4	5
Kdg.	15 – 23	23	24 – 46	47 – 69	70 – 92	93 – 115
1	15 – 23	23	24 – 46	47 – 69	70 – 92	93 – 115
2	16 – 24	24	25 – 48	49 – 72	73 – 96	97 – 120
3	16 – 24	24	25 – 48	49 – 72	73 – 96	97 – 120
4	17 – 25	25	26 – 50	51 – 75	76 – 100	101 – 125
5	17 – 25	25	26 – 50	51 – 75	76 – 100	101 – 125

EMPLOYEE COMPENSATION

Employee compensation methods vary from district to district, but to a large extent, they are driven by employee satisfaction. In this section, we will examine each of the three main employee groups individually: teachers, non-certified personnel, and administrators. However, before discussing compensation models, it is important to understand the concept of salary market philosophy.

- Is it fair for teachers to argue that they should be paid more than auto mechanics because they have a higher level of education?
- Do superintendents in a particular geographic area earning an average of $150,000 have a valid point when they argue that they should be paid more since superintendents in another region of the state average $195,000?
- Is it valid for teachers in one district to select the teacher salary schedule from the highest paying district in the state and demand because they are paid the same because they work just as hard?
- Is the school board fair when it contends during the collective bargaining process that their teachers are too highly paid when the Board selectively chose 10 of the lowest paying school districts in the area for comparison?

The answers, of course, are no. Educators, similar to other professions, are compensated commensurate to what other educators are paid within some logically defined market. This market area usually includes some specific geographic boundaries and type of district (K-8, 9-12, or K-12). Often both the teachers and school boards agree to a defined market during the collective bargaining process.

By way of example, in the school district where I served as superintendent, we had an agreement that the "salary market" for teacher compensation included all the elementary and high school districts in three townships: Evanston, New Trier, and Niles. This helped provide focus during the bargaining process

Defining the market is only the first step in the compensation process. The second is establishing a market philosophy by setting a target for employee compensation in the market area. Some districts have clearly defined market positions such as "We want our employees to be paid at the average of the market." Others may not actually define a market philosophy, but see one emerge as actual salaries are determined.

If I was interpreting the compensation philosophies of these two school districts, I might conclude that Chicago 299 is primarily interested in attracting new teachers since it offers a substantially higher beginning salary but less committed to the career faculty members because of its lower top salary. On the other hand, because of its high MA32 Step 30 salary, Skokie 68's philosophy is probably designed to reward longevity and reduce teacher turnover.

Teacher Compensation

Even though calls for merit plan plans or performance bonuses are increasingly common, teachers are still paid similar to the way they have been paid for decades. That is, they are compensated through teacher salary schedules with salary increases based on experience (steps) and the number of semester graduate credits (lanes) earned. The number of steps and lanes vary, however, from district to district and are usually determined through the collective bargaining process. They are also influenced heavily by the financial position of the school district since a lack of resources may limit the increase the board of education is willing to accept. A sample school district FY 2013-14 teacher salary schedule follows:

TEACHERS' SALARY SCHEDULE 2013-14

	BA		BA+16		MA		MA+8		MA+16		MA+24		MA+32	
Steps	Index	Amount	Index	Amount	Index	Amount	Index	Amount	Index	Amount	Index	Amount	Index	Amount
1	1.00	46,351	1.050	48,669	1.12	51,913	1.14	52,840	1.16	53,767	1.18	54,694	1.20	55,621
2	1.03	47,742	1.080	50,059	1.16	53,767	1.18	54,694	1.20	55,621	1.22	56,548	1.24	57,475
3	1.08	50,059	1.120	51,913	1.21	56,085	1.23	57,012	1.25	57,939	1.27	58,866	1.29	59,793
4	1.13	52,377	1.170	54,231	1.26	58,402	1.28	59,329	1.30	60,256	1.32	61,183	1.34	62,110
5	1.18	54,694	1.220	56,548	1.31	60,720	1.33	61,647	1.35	62,574	1.37	63,501	1.39	64,428
6	1.22	56,548	1.270	58,866	1.37	63,501	1.39	64,428	1.41	65,355	1.43	66,282	1.45	67,209
7	1.27	58,866	1.310	60,720	1.43	66,282	1.45	67,209	1.47	68,136	1.49	69,063	1.51	69,990
8	1.31	60,720	1.350	62,574	1.49	69,063	1.51	69,990	1.53	70,917	1.55	71,844	1.57	72,771
9	1.34	62,110	1.390	64,428	1.55	71,844	1.57	72,771	1.59	73,698	1.61	74,625	1.63	75,552
10	1.37	63,501	1.420	65,818	1.61	74,625	1.63	75,552	1.65	76,479	1.67	77,406	1.69	78,333
11	1.40	64,891	1.450	67,209	1.67	77,406	1.69	78,333	1.71	79,260	1.73	80,187	1.75	81,114
12	1.43	66,282	1.480	68,599	1.73	80,187	1.75	81,114	1.77	82,041	1.79	82,968	1.81	83,895
13	1.45	67,209	1.510	69,990	1.79	82,968	1.81	83,895	1.83	84,822	1.85	85,749	1.87	86,676
14	1.47	68,136	1.540	71,381	1.85	85,749	1.87	86,676	1.89	87,603	1.91	88,530	1.93	89,457
15	1.48	68,599	1.570	72,771	1.92	88,994	1.94	89,921	1.96	90,848	1.98	91,775	2.00	92,702
16	1.49	69,063	1.585	73,466	1.94	89,921	1.96	90,848	1.98	91,775	2.00	92,702	2.02	93,629
17	1.50	69,527	1.600	74,162	1.96	90,848	1.98	91,775	2.00	92,702	2.02	93,629	2.04	94,556
18	1.51	69,990	1.615	74,857	1.98	91,775	2.00	92,702	2.02	93,629	2.04	94,556	2.06	95,483
19	1.52	70,454	1.630	75,552	2.00	92,702	2.02	93,629	2.04	94,556	2.06	95,483	2.08	96,410
20	1.53	70,917	1.645	76,247	2.02	93,629	2.04	94,556	2.06	95,483	2.08	96,410	2.10	97,337
21	1.54	71,381	1.660	76,943	2.04	94,556	2.06	95,483	2.08	96,410	2.10	97,337	2.12	98,264
22	1.55	71,844	1.675	77,638	2.06	95,483	2.08	96,410	2.10	97,337	2.12	98,264	2.14	99,191
23	1.56	72,308	1.690	78,333	2.08	96,410	2.10	97,337	2.12	98,264	2.14	99,191	2.16	100,118
24	1.57	72,771	1.705	79,028	2.10	97,337	2.12	98,264	2.14	99,191	2.16	100,118	2.18	101,045
25	1.58	73,235	1.720	79,724	2.12	98,264	2.14	99,191	2.16	100,118	2.18	101,045	2.20	101,972
26	1.59	73,698	1.735	80,419	2.14	99,191	2.16	100,118	2.18	101,045	2.20	101,972	2.22	102,899
27	1.60	74,162	1.750	81,114	2.16	100,118	2.18	101,045	2.20	101,972	2.22	102,899	2.24	103,826
28	1.61	74,625	1.765	81,810	2.18	101,045	2.20	101,972	2.22	102,899	2.24	103,826	2.26	104,753
29	1.62	75,089	1.780	82,505	2.20	101,972	2.22	102,899	2.24	103,826	2.26	104,753	2.28	105,680
30	1.63	75,552	1.795	83,200	2.22	102,899	2.24	103,826	2.26	104,753	2.28	105,680	2.30	106,607

You probably noticed that along the left side there are 30 steps. Teachers move up one step each year. This is what is referred to as the step increase. One source of confusion and sometimes disagreement in collective bargaining relates to the step increase. Traditionally, teachers do not equate a step change to a raise while school board members do. The reality is that step movement is a raise because it increases a teacher's salary from one year to the next. Even if the salary schedule as a whole did not change, teachers would still receive higher salaries the following year as they moved up a step. Only those at step 30 would not see an increase.

During presentations to the board of education or during contract negotiations, you will hear the term, average cost of step. As part of the budget preparation process or during collective bargaining, school business officials will calculate the average cost of the step increase. This figure represents the average percentage increase to the board for all teachers. It is not uncommon for an average cost of a step increase to be 2% or more. Therefore, without any salary schedule increase, teachers will average 2% higher salaries merely because they moved up a step on the teacher salary schedule.

In addition to steps, teachers' salaries increase if they earn additional graduate study credit. You will notice that our sample teacher salary schedule has seven lanes ranging from BA to MA+32. The number of lanes varies significantly from district to district; however, they too have additional salary increases associated with them.

Therefore, teachers who move up a step and earn enough graduate course credit to change lanes would receive raises for both even if the schedule stayed the same.

To illustrate this further, let's take a look at the percentage increase a teacher would receive on our sample schedule even if the schedule remained the same from year to year. For calculation purposes, here are our assumptions.

- Teacher moved from BA Step 4 to MA Step 5; and,
- The salary schedule as a whole remained the same

Table 8.2
Salary Increase Cost Comparison

FY 2014 Salary	FY 2015 Salary	Salary Increase	Salary Increase
$52,377	$60,720	$8,343	15.9%

Isn't this interesting? This particular teacher would receive a 15.9% increase without any schedule change. The FY2015 salary would even be higher if the entire salary schedule increased.

Finally, you may also be familiar with the term "schedule increase." Traditionally, teacher schedules in their entirety increase annually. When the complete schedule increases, this is referred to as a schedule increase.

Most teachers actually receive at least two separate annual increases: schedule and step. Some also qualify for a lane-related increase if they earn additional graduate course credit. Is it any wonder that when contract negotiations heat up and percent increase figures are discussed by the Board and teachers was well as written about in local newspapers that there is some confusion?

In addition to the steps and lanes on our sample schedule, you also see something called the index. Many but not all salary schedules are built on indexes. When salary schedules are distributed to teachers, sometimes the indexes are not included because they can be a source of confusion for those not familiar with salary schedule structures. What most teachers really want to know is – "What is my salary for the year"?

Administrators need to understand salary schedule indexing. In the schedule above, the index represents the percentage that any point on the salary schedule is higher than the base (BA Step1) salary. To illustrate this, look at BA Step I. The salary for this step is $46,351. BA Step 2 has an index of 1.03. To calculate the salary for BA Step 2, you multiple the base salary $46,351 by the index for the step (1.03) resulting in a BA Step 2 salary of $47,742.

$46,351 X 1.03 = $47,742

The same process is used to establish each point on the salary schedule. One advantage of this system is that a district can negotiate a base salary then create a spreadsheet with built in indexes to almost instantly create a salary schedule.

A salary schedule indexing system can provide valuable insights into a school district's salary philosophy. If you study the indexing pattern in Teachers' Salary Schedule 2013-14, what conclusion might you draw about this school district's salary philosophy? Here are a few that I would suggest. The school district:

- Encourages teachers to earn their masters degree. Note the large increase in index points between the BA+16 and MA lanes.
- Encourages increased educational training up to the MA level but does not value it as much beyond that since index point increases are much smaller.
- Strives to increase teachers' salaries more quickly during their first 15 years, possibly to achieve earlier comparability in the market area. Beyond that point, index points only increase .01 to .02 annually.
- Encourages employee longevity. Not only does it have a 30 step scale, but the top salary is substantial.

You may want to examine your own district's salary schedule to see what patterns you can identify.

Another common feature of teacher compensation programs is the inclusion of longevity provisions. These are usually additional salary amounts, which are added to teachers' salaries the year after they have reached the last step on the schedule. These are established during the collective bargaining process and are generally listed as a footnote on the salary schedule. If, for example, the district teacher salary schedule above had a $500 per year longevity provision, a teacher with 31 years of service in the MA32 lane would be paid $108,882.60 (Illinois Teacher Retirement System, 2012). Longevity increases are cumulative and continue as long as the teacher is employed.

Finally, it is important to recognize that not only does the teacher salary schedule approach have a long history in public education, but the Illinois state legislature has all but ensured that the present model will continue with passage of the Illinois Labor Relations Act of 1984. This law requires school boards to bargain collectively with teacher unions. In essence, it narrows the compensation model options by requiring agreement from teachers before any change can be made in teacher salaries (Braun, 2010).

Emerging Trends in Teacher Compensation

As noted earlier, teachers generally continue to be compensated based on traditional salary schedules. However, new compensation trends are beginning to emerge. Once unthinkable, elimination of the traditional teacher salary schedule is now a realistic topic of teacher negotiations. As the US economy has deteriorated and funding for public education has tightened, school boards have begun winning concessions on teacher compensation during collective bargaining.

Some school districts such as Addison School District 4 and Wheaton Community School District 200 have successfully negotiated what is termed a hard freeze. That is, in these school districts, teachers have agreed to forgo both schedule and step increases for a year.

In other school districts such as Des Plaines School District 62 and Gurnee School District 56, teachers agreed to a soft freeze. Under this approach, the schedule remains the same but teachers receive only a schedule increase.

In still others such as Skokie School District 68 and Skokie School District 73.5, teachers receive either a specific dollar amount or fixed percentage bonus for the year. During the following school year, they are placed back on the existing salary schedule.

In still others such as Highland Park Township High School District 113, the latest contract creates a two tiered system. New faculty members advance a half step while current teachers move up a full step.

Trends such as these are becoming more common. An important question to consider is - Do these teacher compensation models signal a new trend or are they merely short-term aberrations?

Non-Certified Personnel

Non-certified personnel (support staff) compensation models tend to be less structured than those of teachers. Even though they enjoy the same collective bargaining rights as teachers, a smaller percent of support staff groups tend to form unions. Historically, they have not sought the same level of unionization as teachers. They also tend to be smaller groups, which were not initially as universally organized as were teachers by national level associations such as the American Federation of Teachers or the National Education Association. Support staff may either affiliate with teachers' unions or form their own.

Although some school districts compensate support staff using a salary schedule model, others are paid primarily on an hourly basis or through some version of a merit-based plan. Others receive annual salaries not tied directly to schedules. Therefore, you will find a variety of compensation models, often primarily a function of local past practices and tradition.

Finally, one common misunderstanding among school administrators is that salaried support staff members are exempt from the overtime pay provisions of the Fair Labor Standards Act. Even if employees are salaried, they are entitled to overtime pay unless they meet the legal standards for exempt status (Braun, 2010).

Administrative Compensation

In Illinois, administrators are management. As such, their salaries are set at the discretion of the board of education. For the most part, administrators need an Illinois Type 75 General Administrative certificate. However, certain employees in some districts, such as psychologists or deans of students, are not part of a bargaining unit nor required to hold an administrative certificate. They may, however, be compensated under the administrative classification.

Administrative compensation models vary from school district to school district. Several of the most common approaches are discussed below.

Administrative Salary Schedules. Although Illinois administrators are not permitted to bargain collectively because they are classified as management employees, school boards may chose to cooperate with administrators as a group as occurs in Chicago 299 (Chicago Public Schools, 2008) . Under this approach, a salary schedule model is used to establish compensation by administrative positions.

Across the Board Increases. Another common compensation model is some form of across the board salary increases. Sometimes the percentage increase is equal to that of other employee groups. Under this approach, administrators typically receive the same percentage increase given to other employee groups such as teachers. However, even with an across the board model, it is not uncommon for boards of education to make exceptions for certain administrators who are viewed as underpaid. The term "catch up" is used to describe a special additional one-time salary increase.

Merit Increases. Unlike teachers, administrators may be compensated under some version of a merit pay plan. Whether this takes the form of linking administrators' salary increases to performance indicators or the awarding of a bonus, merit plans tend to be individual in nature. In many instances, actual salary increases under merit plans may be tied to meeting broad goals or even the reputation of the administrator as perceived by the board of education and/or superintendent rather than exact quantitative criteria. Nonetheless, this model is common in Illinois.

Unique Plans. In addition to the above approaches, school boards may adopt any other compensation model they choose. In one district in which I served, administrators were paid based upon their position in the salary market. The compensation philosophy was to pay administrators toward the low end of the salary market range for their position when they were hired. Then, as they performed satisfactorily over a number of years, their salaries would increase to the point that they ultimately reached the third quartile of their market.

Quartile refers to the position of the salary in the market. For example, if you had a market composed of 19 administrators whose salaries were ranked from the bottom to the top. The 5th salary from the bottom would be the 1st quartile, the 10th would represent the second quartile or median while the 15th would be the 3rd quartile. Therefore, at the 3rd quartile, three-quarters of the salaries in the market would be lower.

Under this model, each year an administrator's salary would be compared to a quartile distribution for that position in the market. Any administrator at the 3rd quartile of their market would receive a market-based increase. Those who fell below the 3rd quartile would receive an additional "catch up" increase depending upon their market position. For example, if an administrator's salary fell in the 1st quartile (the lowest salary up to the first quartile), the person would receive an additional 3% salary increase. From the 1st quartile to the 2nd quartile or median, the increase would be 2%; while above the median to the 3rd quartile, the salary raise would increase 1%. However, if an administrator's salary exceeded the 3rd quartile, the person would have 1% deducted from the market increase since the compensation philosophy goal was to pay administrators at the 3rd quartile of the market.

Through this process, administrators were well paid but not the highest. Since the system was market data-driven versus arbitrary, it was perceived by administrators as fair and equitable. It is also important to note that the superintendent could recommend a smaller or even no raise for any administrator not performing to district standards.

EMPLOYEE BENEFITS

Frequently, the second largest reoccurring district expenditure is for employee benefits. It is not unusual for benefit costs to be 10% or more of overall expenditures. This is not surprising since one of the widely recognized advantages of a career in public education has traditionally been excellent benefits.

The most common general employee benefits include:

1. Insurance
    a. Health
    b. Dental
    c. Vision
    d. Term life
    e. Disability

2. Paid Time Off
    a. Sick days
    b. Personal or business days
    c. Vacation: administrators and non-certified employees

Depending upon the employee group, these benefits may vary. Most often, requiring employees to pay at least a portion of any insurance premium is considered sound policy. Without some cost, employees may automatically accept a benefit even if it is not needed, thereby driving up district costs. For example, employees may be covered by their spouses' health insurance plans, but also take advantage of the district's insurance if offered at no cost. Under the other hand, if employees have to pay a portion of the premium, they may elect to decline district coverage.

Another advantage of shared premium costs is that it encourages employee groups to participate in studying ways to reduce premiums (Kersten & Dada, 2005). School districts may collaborate with employees to form committees designed to study insurance programs in order to find ways to reduce costs while maintaining acceptable coverage levels. Since both the district and employees benefit from premium reductions, this can be a win-win situation for both. In times of tight finances, school districts are wise to look for such strategies to reduce overall benefit costs.

HEALTH CARE OPTIONS

Do you remember the first time you were asked to select from an array of healthcare plans? If you are similar to many employees, you were probably confused. You may have had to choose from a list of option ranging from traditional fee for service plans to health maintenance organization (HMO) with varying benefit and premium cost levels. Although an in-depth understanding of each may be necessary for school business officials, what you really need is a basic understanding of the various options. In this section, I will summarize the key elements of each. To fully understand the differences in your local school district plans including options even within the categories below, you will want to contact the school districts insurance specialist.

Health Maintenance Organization

Usually the lowest cost healthcare plan for both the school district and the employee is the HMO. Often referred to as a managed care plan, participants select a primary care physician within the Health Maintenance Organization (HMO) network who initiates medical treatment as necessary which may include referral to HMO approved specialist as needed. The primary advantages of an HMO include:

- Lower premiums;
- No deductibles;
- Low co-pays for services; and,
- No claim filing paperwork.

Because of the reduced costs, those electing an HMO lose the flexibility to receive treatment from medical professionals not part of the HMO network (Kersten & Dada, 2005).

Preferred Provider Option

A popular employee insurance option is the Preferred Provider Option (PPO). Unlike the HMO, PPOs allow employees to seek medical treatment directly from any healthcare professionals, including specialists, who are part of the PPO network. For this flexibility, those electing the PPO can expect higher annual deductibles and increased out-of-pocket costs. Also, participants must ensure that the doctors they choose are approved by the PPO or be willing to pay substantially more for medical care. However, in most areas, the number of doctors participating in PPOs is usually quite high (Kersten & Dada, 2005).

Fee for Services

A health insurance option which is disappearing from the market is the traditional Fee for Services plan. Under this option, employees have complete freedom of choice for both doctors and hospitals but must complete claim paperwork. However, the high cost of premiums in many districts has eliminated this as an option.

Flexible Spending Accounts and Dependent Care Assistance Plans

Most school districts allow employees to take advantage of an Internal Revenue Service approved option to shelter a portion of their income with a specific limit from federal and state taxes to pay for specific healthcare costs including health insurance premiums, medical and dental care including prescriptions and even certain over-the-counter items through a Flexible Spending Account (FSA). Employees can contribute up to $2,500.

A Dependent Care Assistance Plan (DCAP) allows employees to shelter up to $5000 annually for childcare costs. One word of caution – employees must "use" or "loose" the amount sheltered within 14.5 months of the beginning of the annual FSA period. DCAT funds must be used within 12 months (Kersten & Dada, 2005).

Health Reimbursement Account

School districts are also authorized to offer Health Reimbursement Account (HRA) to employees. This benefit option, which is a specified dollar amount provided by the Board of Education, is usually negotiated as part of collective bargaining. Similar to FSAs, employees may use these tax free funds to pay healthcare costs. School districts often provide these as a way to provide an incentive to participants to accept higher deductibles accompanied by annual lower premiums. Since the lower premium costs benefit both the board and employees while allowing participants to use their HRA to pay the increased deductibles, they can be a win-win for everyone (Kersten & Dada, 2005).

Health Savings Account

An increasing popular insurance-related benefit is the Health Savings Account (HSA). Although it is probably not appropriate for those who require regular medical care such as families with children or those with high levels of healthcare needs, employees who do not seek healthcare very often may find it attractive. What distinguishes an HSA from a FSA and HRA is that it is actually owned and controlled by the employee not the school district but is managed through the district. Consequently, participants may carry over HSA funds indefinitely. They are also free to invest HSA funds in a wide range of options including mutual funds. HSAs are typically funded by employees and/or school districts with tax free dollars. (Kersten & Dada, 2005). HSAs must also be offered in conjunction with a regular healthcare plan with deductible minimums of $1,200 for single and $2,400 for family coverage (U.S. Department of the Treasury, 2012).

REDUCING HEALTH CARE COSTS

As school districts struggle to find ways to reduce expenditures, they often look toward healthcare costs, which traditionally increase at a rate far exceeding inflation. In fact, the Kaiser Family Foundation (2012) reports that the average family premium was 113% higher in 2011 than 2001. From 2010 to 2011, the average family premium increase was 9% while the single premium grew by 8%. As a consequence, school administrators must look for ways to reduce health insurance related costs. Several strategies a colleague and I proposed included the following (Kersten & Dada, 2005).

Educate Yourself on Costs

An important first step is learning as much as possible about all aspects of health insurance. Without a sound understanding of healthcare components and costs, little substantial progress can be made.

Analyze Premium Expenditures and Identify Areas for Cost Containment

Since most administrators are not insurance experts, they must rely on industry experts for advice on ways to contain costs. As a result, some consult their present insurance cooperative manager or insurance broker or employ a cost reduction specialist with a high level of industry expertise who will study such areas as:

- Present plan performance;
- Prescription drug program;
- Cost-containment opportunities with employee groups; and,
- Opportunities to negotiate commissions/fixed fees, direct medical services, and claim management.

Partner with Employees

Since both employers and employees benefit from reduction in premium costs, a good starting point for school administrators is to suggest the formation of a joint administration/employee benefit committee led by an insurance consultant to review the current health insurance program and recommend changes that may reduce costs without significantly reducing benefits.

Manage Prescription Plans Aggressively

According to the Kaiser Family Foundation, prescription drugs represent 10% of total healthcare costs (Kaiser Family Foundation, 2012). Therefore, examining ways to reduce these costs is important. Often, by adjusting co-pays for prescription drugs, school districts and employee may be able to reduce medical insurance premiums substantially.

Promote Healthier Lifestyles

School administrators may be able to reduce insurance costs by promoting life-style changes. Although the results may not be immediate, they may have an effect over a longer period of time. Some suggestions include:

- Providing wellness screening;
- Offering smoking cessation programs;
- Providing incentives for weight loss and smoking cessation;
- Working with fitness clubs to provide membership specials;
- Sponsoring fitness activities;
- Communicating disease management information; and,
- Highlighting the wellness features of healthcare plans.

OTHER EMPLOYEES INSURANCE OFFERINGS

In addition to health insurance, school district employees may offer several other insurance-related benefits including dental, vision, life, and disability. Premium and benefit levels are typically locally determined, often as an outcome of the collective bargaining process. Dental insurance generally provides full coverage for cleaning while both dental and vision plans pay a percentage of related medical costs. Life insurance usually provided upon death a flat dollar amount or a percentage related to income level. Finally, employees who elect disability insurance are provided a percentage of their income for an extended period when they are unable to work due to illness or injury.

PAID TIME OFF

Finally, a true benefit of a career in education in contrast to the business world is the number of work days. A widely recognized benefit whether you are an administrator, teacher, or support person is the increased number of days off. Not only do school district employees receive additional paid holidays, but many have extended time off during winter, spring, and summer breaks. Also, school employees are provided generous paid sick leave allocations, often accompanied by unlimited unused sick leave accumulation.

It is also common for school districts to allow employees two or more days annually for either personal and/or business use. Twelve month administrators and classified personnel usually receive vacation days in addition to regular school holidays.

BENEFIT PLAN VARIANCES

One area in which administrators are often rewarded beyond other employee groups is in fringe benefits. As with compensation, fringe benefit levels are traditionally tied to an administrative benefit market. Because administrators are usually the smallest employee group and represent the board of education, they typically receive higher board subsidies for insurance premiums, in many instances 100%. In addition, administrators may also be provided travel allowances and conference cost reimbursements not generally available to other employee groups.

Most school district attorneys will recommend that the board of education establish a separate written administrative benefit plan to clearly delineate all fringe benefits. This approach not only establishes a clear understanding of benefits offered but provides continuity during times of administrator and board transition.

TOTAL COMPENSATION

Employees often view total compensation models as equitable since all employees receive the same dollar amount, irrespective of their personal situations. Everyone is treated the same, unlike traditional benefit plans where some employees receive a great deal more in fringe benefit dollars from the district based on their benefit choices. If, for example, a teacher's spouse has a benefit plan that provides family health insurance, the teacher may choose to use the district's fringe benefit dollars for additional salary or a 403(b).

The negative aspect of total compensation for employees is that they assume the risk of premium increases much more directly. Also, insurance premiums often increase at a much greater rate than salaries. As a result, teachers over time may find a larger portion of their pay allocated to pay insurance premiums.

For school district boards, a total compensation approach can be attractive since it places a greater portion of the risk for premium increases on the shoulders of the employees. Also, district costs are more predictable since benefit amounts are fixed.

RETIREMENT PLANS

One of the most substantial public education employee benefits is access to a defined benefit retirement plan – lifetime retirement income. Unlike much of the business world which has shifted from defined benefit models to defined contribution plans such as the 401(k), an retirement investment account owned by individual employees into which typically both employees and employers contribute some amount. Since Illinois public school employees have defined benefit retirement plans, they earn generous retirement annuities for life. The three public school retirement systems in Illinois are the Teacher Retirement System (TRS), Chicago Teachers Pension Fund (CTPF), and Illinois Municipal Retirement Fund (IMRF).

Teacher Retirement System (TRS)

School district employees, who are required to hold Illinois certification for their positions, including administrators, are members of TRS (Teachers' Retirement System, 2012). Since this is a state-funded pension system, the State of Illinois contributes substantially to TRS annually. In addition, both employers and employees contribute a percentage linked to employee salaries. The FY2013 contribution rate for employees was 9.4% of gross salary, while employers contributed 0.58%. In addition, TRS members also contribute an additional 0.92% and employers 0.69% for FY13 to help fund the Teachers' Health Insurance Security (THIS) Fund. TRS participants are eligible to retire at age 60 under the regular program with 10 years of service and at 62 with 5 years. Under certain circumstances, which will be discussed later, retirement may occur before age 60.

TRS is a formula driven system through which retirement annuities are calculated based on a person's years of service and final average salary. For most teachers, the formula is fairly simple. For each year of employment, teachers earn 2.2% in service credit. Therefore, teachers who retire with 20 years of service have accrued 44% toward the pension formula. If they retire with 35 years of service credit (the maximum allowed for the pension calculation), their percentage is 75%. Retirees who have 34 years of service (34 years X 2.2% a year = 74.8%) must participate in the Early Retirement Option (ERO) to avoid a penalty.

In addition to calculating the service credit percentage, a final average salary is determined by taking the salaries of the highest four consecutive years in the teacher's final ten and dividing it by four. For example, if the employee's final four highest consecutive salaries were $69,000, $73,000, $77,000, and $81,000, the average annual salary would be $75,000.

Once the percentage and average final salary are calculated, doing the math is quite simple. However, in order to retire without a penalty, teachers need to either be 60 years of age or have 35 full years of service credit. It is important to note that TRS employees may accumulate up to 340 unused and uncompensated sick days for up to two years of service credit.

To illustrate a simple pension, let's assume the teacher:

- Is 60 years old at retirement (No penalty calculation required)
- Has 35 years of service and therefore the 75% maximum service credit
- Had an average final salary of $75,000

The formula is:

Percentage Earned for Years of Service X Average Final Salary = Annual Pension

75% (.75) X $75,000 = $67,500

In addition to the annual pension, retirees receive a 3% pension increase each January. However, retirees do not begin collecting the 3% increase until the January following their 61st birthday. The good news, though, is that the increase is retroactive to the date of retirement. As a result, most retirees can expect a substantial pension increase at that time, particularly if they retired at 55.

Early Retirement Option (ERO)

In Illinois, teachers may retire if they are at least 55 years of age by December 31 of their retirement year and have earned a minimum of 20 years of service credit. Thus some teachers choose to retiree before age 60 without maximum service credit. Under this scenario, teachers have two options. They can retire either with or without participating in the state's Early Retirement Option (ERO).

With ERO

Another option available to teachers 55 and over who have a minimum of 20 years of service credit but are not yet 60 years of age is the Early Retirement Option (ERO). Under ERO, TRS employees may retire before age 60 with less than 35 years of service without a pension reduction if both they and their employer pay a fee to TRS. Employees pay 11.5% times their highest salary for each year they are under 60 or 35 years of service, whichever is less. Employers contribute 23.5% times the highest salary for each year an employee is under 60. ERO is only guaranteed until 2013. Prior to that, the Illinois legislature will review ERO to determine if it will continue. If not, the retirement age without penalty (pension reduction) will be 60.

To illustrate the cost of ERO to both the retiree and the school board, let's consider an example. Our assumptions are that the retiree:

- Is 55 years old;
- Has 28 years of service; and,
- Has a final highest salary of $90,000.

Given these assumptions, in order for this teacher to retire, the individual would be required to pay $51,750. This is because the teacher is 5 years under age 60. As a result, the teacher is assessed 57.5% (11.5% X 5 years) of their $90,000 salary. The school board would have a much larger assessment, $105,750 (117.5% X $90,000). One point worth noting is that even though the teacher has the option for ERO, the school board by law does not. It must pay the required fee to TRS if the teacher chooses ERO. However, the school board does have the right to limit the number of employees who can retire annually under ERO to 10% of those eligible. Nonetheless, the costs for boards of education, especially if several employees choose to retire in a specific year, can be a substantial.

Without ERO

A good question to consider is – what impact does retiring without ERO have on a person's pension? Unfortunately, the effect is substantial. Retirees are subject to a steep pension reduction, 1/2 percent per month (six percent a year) for each month they are under 60 if they have less than 35 years of service credit. Although the retiree may avoid the early retirement fee associated with ERO, the pension reduction may minimize the viability of early retirement. For example, a person who would otherwise has a pension of $50K and retires at age 55 without ERO is penalized 30% resulting in an annual pension of $35K.

Salary Increase Maximums

One other provision that is important to consider is a relatively recent change in the maximum amount a person's salary can increase during the final four years of employment without the board of education accruing a substantial penalty. At the present time, the limit is 6% a year, which virtually eliminated the 20% bonuses that had become common in certain areas of the state. Boards of education will be very reluctant to approve any teacher or administrator contract which exceeds this level.

Optional Credit

Another important TRS provision you should be aware of is optional service credit. TRS members may earn service credit even when not working in a teacher certified position in an Illinois public school. TRS members may earn service credit for such experiences as military service, employer-approved leaves of absence related to such reasons as childbirth, and certain out-of-state teaching.

Survivor Benefit

As part of their TRS contributions, members pay for survivor benefits. Under this TRS provision, spouses of retirees who have passed away can elect to receive one-half of the deceased member's pension as well as the 3% annual increases for life.

In this section, we examined a typical, non-complex retirement calculations. However, a full discussion of all possible factors was unrealistic. To understand the system in greater detail or relate it to your personal situation, you are encouraged to either visit the TRS website at http://trs.illinois.gov or call their office.

CHICAGO TEACHERS PENSION FUND (CTPF)

The CTPF is similar in many respects to TRS including the formula-driven retirement calculation which uses salary and service credit to determine the actual pension (Chicago Teacher Pension Fund, 2012). However, there are some significant differences. These include:

- A pension contribution of 2% of regular pay from the employee and 7% from the Chicago Board of Education;
- No limits on salary for the pension calculation;
- A maximum of 244 unused, uncompensated sick days toward service credit;
- At the present time, the Chicago Public School District 299 Board of Education does not offer ERO. The last time it was available, CPS teachers could retire with a reduced pension if they were at least 55 and had 20 years of service;
- The option to retire at age 60 without a reduced pension with a minimum of 20 years service credit; and,
- A non-retroactive 3% annual pension increase, which begins after a retiree has reached 61 of age and been retired for at least one year.

The list above summarizes some of the most significant differences. To understand the CTPF provisions more fully, you can access their website at http://ctpf.org or contact their Chicago office.

ILLINOIS MUNICIPAL RETIREMENT FUND (IMRF)

School employees who are not required to hold an Illinois teaching certificate and work 600 or more hours a year for at least 8 years are eligible for an IMRF pension (Illinois Municipal Retirement Fund, 2012). It is interesting to note that this is a state endorsed independent pension system, which also includes other municipal workers such as city and park district employees. Only the employer and employee, not the state, contribute to IMRF.

The minimum retirement age is 55. Employees who retire between 55 and 60 with less than 30 years service have their pensions reduced by 1/4% for each month they are under 60. If they have 35 years of service but less than 40, their pensions are reduced the lesser of 1/4% per month under age 60 or 1/4% per month under 35 years of service.

Under IMRF, employees' pensions are calculated similar to TRS through a formula which includes two factors: a service credit percentage determined by an employee's experience and an average salary based on the highest consecutive 48 months in the employees final ten years. Similar to TRS, retirees receive a life-long pension.

Employees contribute 4.5% of their income, while the employer's payment is actuarially determined by IMRF. Members may also use one year of accrued uncompensated sick leave (240 days) for service credit.

An employee's pension can vary significantly based on years of IMRF experience, age at retirement, and salary history. However, to illustrate how the pension formula works, let's consider an employee who has:

- 40 years of service (Number of years of service needed for a maximum pension of 75% of average salary)
- An average annual salary of $50,000 (Average annual salary based on the highest 48 consecutive months in the last 10 years)

The pension formula is:

- Percentage accrued for years of service X Average final salary = Annual Pension
- 75% (.75) X $50,000 = $38,000 Annual Pension

In addition, three other provisions are worth noting. First, a retiree's spouse receives one half of the retiree's pension for life in the event of death. Also, a 3% pension increase tied to the retiree's initial retirement annuity is added each January following retirement.

Retirees also receive additional annual compensation under what IMRF calls the 13th check program. The 2011 13th payment was 44.419% of the monthly pension. The amount varies from year to year but was designed to partially offset the fixed annual pension increase, which is not cumulative as it is under TRS. IMRF employers contribute 0.62% of their payrolls to fund this payment. To calculate the retiree payment, IMRF takes the total amount contributed by employers and divides it by the June benefit payments to retirees (Illinois Municipal Retirement Fund, 2012). To understand in greater detail these provisions as well as how an IMRF pension is calculated including the percentage rates for various years of service, please see the fund's website at http://www.imrf.org.

RECIPROCAL SYSTEMS

Under the Illinois Retirement Reciprocal Act, retirees from 11 different systems may combine service credit toward retirement (Chicago Teacher Pension Fund, 2012). This provision allows, for example, teachers who earn service credit under IMRF as teacher assistants to combine this with their TRS credit when calculating their retirement annuities even though a portion of their pension will be paid by each system.

CHANGES IN FUTURE PENSIONS

As of January 1, 2011 a new two tier pension system took effective for public school employees. Current members of TRS, CTPF, IMRF, and other reciprocal systems (Tier I) are not affected by the changes. However, employees hired after January 1, 2011 are subject to Tier II regulations (Teachers' Retirement System, 2012).

These changes are substantial. In fact, Tier II hires can expect significantly reduced retirement benefits. Although the impact of the changes is a long way off for most new hires, an understanding of future retirement benefits is essential for long-term financial planning.

The key changes for Tier I include:

- Full benefits beginning at age 67 rather than age 60;
- An option to retire at 62 but with a 6% pension discount for every year under age 67;
- The use of the highest consecutive 8 years salaries for the average salary portion of the pension calculation;
- A $110,800 maximum final average 2012 salary, which is indexed. It may be increase annually as the CPI increases, but is not compounde1;
- An annual, non-compounded cost of living increase of one half of the CPI but not more than 3%;
- A 66% survivor benefit level; and,
- Tighter post-retirement restrictions on employment in any of the reciprocal systems.

ADVISING EMPLOYEES

As you can see from our discussion, each of the retirement systems is somewhat complex. Administrators need to understand the basic provisions in order to work with boards of education and employee groups. However, they also need to exercise caution when advising individual employees. Retirement system personnel have the knowledge necessary to calculate retirement annuities and are the only ones authorized to answer employee questions. Although it is appropriate to have preliminary discussions with employees about retirement, responsible administrators will always refer employees to their respective retirement systems for advice and any potential pension calculations.

OTHER EMPLOYEES RETIREMENT SAVINGS OPTIONS

In addition to the defined benefit retirement plans, most school districts will provide voluntary access to defined contribution plans in which employees may participate to supplement their pensions. These are individually owned investment accounts to which employees contribute a portion of their regular income. Since they are retirement accounts, most employees are not able to withdraw funds without a substantial tax penalty until they are 59 ½ years old. The three most well known options potentially available to K-12 public school employees are the regular 403(b), Roth 403(b), and 457 deferred compensation plans (Lincoln Investments, 2012).

403(b)

The most widely offered defined contribution plan in Illinois public school districts is the 403(b), a tax deferred retirement plan. Offered through the school district, employees contribute pre-tax dollars to an investment account with a district authorized investment or annuity company through a payroll reduction agreement. The investment account earnings grow tax deferred until withdrawal (usually after retirement) but no sooner than age 59 ½ or as a result of separation of service at 55. Fund withdrawals are subject to the employee's regular income tax rate (Internal Revenue Services, 2012). Participants typically have several investment options through mutual funds companies or annuities issued by insurance companies. Employees for 2012 may contribute up to $17,000 of income or $22,500 if 50 or older (Lincoln Investments, 2012).

Roth 403(b)

Another type of defined contribution plan which became available in 2005 is the Roth 403(b) which some school districts make available to employees. The Roth is largely the same as the regular 403(b) with one important exception. Employees make after-tax contributions; however, all qualifying distributions are tax free. Depending upon their personal circumstances such as age and projected income tax level at retirement, participants need to weigh which type of 403(b) makes the most sense for their individual circumstances (Internal Revenue Service, 2012).

457 Deferred Compensation

A third type is the 457 Deferred Compensation plan, a tax deferred retirement savings vehicle very similar to the 403(b). Contribution levels are the same as the 403(b); however, one important consideration is that an employee may participate in both a 403(b) and a 457 simultaneously thereby doubling the amount they can invest. For example, teachers 50 years of age or older with sufficient income can invest up to $45,000 annually. A 457 also provides opportunities to withdraw funds penalty free prior to 59½ in certain situations (Lincoln Investments, 2012).

Each of the three optional retirement savings plans offers the potential for employees to plan efficiently and effectively for retirement. However, similar to any investment, these are not without risk especially since they are often highly invested in the stock market. As of January 1, 2009, school districts assumed more additional responsibilities for 403(b) plans including providing information to employees and oversight for employee investments and fee assessments.

SUMMARY

In Chapter 8, we have examined four personnel-related areas including staffing patterns, compensation models, fringe benefits including healthcare options, and retirement planning. Each of these impacts the financial position of the district. School administrators must be well informed in each area if they are to be an efficient and effective school-level and district leaders.

Chapter 9

Financial Distress

Although many school districts are able to maintain a reasonable financial position by maximizing their regular sources of revenue, controlling expenditures, and utilizing long-term financial planning strategies, some school districts cannot. Even though they do their best to maintain a stable educational program with limited resources, ultimately many arrive at a point where sound fiscal management alone is just not enough. This is especially true for school districts under PTELL restrictions where revenues do not keep pace with escalating expenditures. For those districts, school boards must find additional revenues and/or expenditure reductions, usually a daunting task.

The most realistic solution for school districts with eroding financial positions is to pass an operating fund tax increase. This requires school boards to ask district voters to increase property taxes through a referendum. All that is required is that a majority of registered voters in the school district vote "yes" for the referendum.

While some districts solve their immediate financial problems through referendum, others unfortunately fail referenda after referenda. As a result, these school boards have little or no choice but to watch their financial positions deteriorate to the point that the school district finds itself in severe financial crisis. When school district finances reach the stage where no further staffing, program, or service cuts are realistic, the district finds itself teetering on the brink of financial crisis.

In this chapter, we will explore both of these scenarios: seeking additional property tax revenue through a referendum and the process legislated in Illinois to respond to imminent school district insolvency.

REFERENDUM CHALLENGES

Although a property tax increase is an effective revenue enhancement strategy, passing one is a substantial challenge. In today's anti-tax, and in particular, anti-property tax environment, school boards and administrators face an uphill battle to convince taxpayers to increase school funding. Recently, my wife and I went to dinner with some old friends, both of whom were retired. Since this was an election year, the conversation naturally turned to politics as we lamented the ongoing barrage of candidate commercials. At one point I asked them who they supported for office. Even I was surprised by the answer I received since I had always seen my friends as good supporters of education. One of them responded, "Anyone who won't raise my taxes." This experience reminded me that school administrators and board members can never afford to take educational support for granted. Rather, they must listen carefully to public opinion. Unfortunately, my friend's response is typical of how many of our constituents feel.

The reality for school board members and administrators is that winning public support for additional revenues will continue to be a tremendous challenge. Consider this. Since 1990, an average of only 36% percent of operating fund referenda, including those asking to increase the limiting rate, have succeeded (IASB Newsletter, 2010). As recently as April 2011, only 41% of questions to raise school district tax rates or to issue bonds were approved (IASA Newsletter, 2011). Given these realities, school district leaders need to understand the factors which contribute to this anti-tax sentiment if they plan to execute a successful referendum campaign.

FACTORS AFFECTING REFERENDUM SUCCESS

As school leaders plan for a referendum campaign, the ability to recognize the obstacles they will face is critical. A low key, non-publicized referendum approach will not likely succeed. Rather, referendum committees need to convince a wide variety of constituents, often with very different and strongly held positions, of the importance of a tax increase. This raises the question – What factors affect referendum campaigns?

Probably the most common factor is the general public's perception that taxes are too high. Strike up a conversation with your neighbors about taxes and, in particular, property taxes and I am sure you will hear a great deal of consternation. We see this sentiment echoed during local, state, and federal elections around, which politicians regularly ratchet up the anti-tax message.

An additional factor is the public's perception of the quality of education. Since at least the publication of A Nation at Risk in 1983 which described the perceived shortcomings of our public schools and placed substantial blame for perceived failing on both educators and our educational system, public education has been under national scrutiny. Again and again, we read about the lack of student achievement including declining student performance against international competition. We also hear education opponents arguing that adequate public school funding is already provided if only we used these resources properly. Often these discussions, which can be perceived as a partisan attack on public education, are driven by the media and centered on the need to set higher standards for teachers, administrators, and students. This intense media scrutiny and barrage of negatively-focused reports, as well as federal legislation such as No Child Left Behind, portray our educational system as broken (Beyer & Johnson, 2005).

Another reality is that we live in a society that is me-centered. Let me relate an experience, which illustrates my point. As superintendent, it was not usual for me to be confronted by groups of parents who employed high pressure tactics to demand special programs or services for their children, even if this meant that other children were negatively affected. One such event immediately comes to mind. A husband and wife, who considered themselves school-community activists, wanted their children's bus stop changed. Their two children had to walk less than a block in a quiet suburban neighborhood to catch the bus. They felt this was inconvenient, particularly in winter, and demanded that the stop be re-located in front of their home.

The business manager and I met with them to discuss their request. After reviewing all pertinent data, we explained to them that we could not move the stop since it would mean a section of the route would have to be revised, which would add additional route time. We also pointed out that other children would be inconvenienced by having to walk over from another street. Their response was that they did not care about the route length or other children. They paid taxes and were influential PTA members and their children should be accommodated. When we did not make the change, they threatened to take the issue to the school board and PTA. Over the next few years, they continued to create ongoing controversy using this event to stir others issues.

The important lesson here is not the actual decision made, but the fact that administrators regularly deal with some individuals who are "me" focused, rather than willing to consider the greater good. Similar to these parents, when presented with a tax increase request, a significant portion of the population may ask – "What is best for me?" A stumbling block in any referendum campaign is attempting to convince individuals who will not benefit directly from the tax increase that it is in the best interest of the community even if it means that they pay higher property taxes. What is somewhat ironic in my example above is that these parents would actually be referendum supporters since their children would personally benefit from increased school district revenue. However, what might their position be in a few years after their children are grown?

Beside parent special interest groups, referendum planners must research community demographics. Traditionally, those who benefit from a referendum such as parents and employees will vote "yes" at a higher rate the others. However, referendum planners need to keep in mind that not all parents will be supporters. What is important to remember is that communities are primarily comprised of individuals who have little interest in the day-to-day activities of the school.

One such group is taxpayers who either have no children or whose children no longer attend district schools. In one district where I served as an administrator, this group represented almost 80% of eligible voters.

By way of example, let me relate one more story. Several years ago, I had a wealthy friend who I would describe as reasonably community-minded. He owned a very successful business. His children had all been "school stars" both academically and athletically. He had nothing but good things to say about the local school system, which his children attended.

One day, after they graduated, our school district went to referendum. As an educator, I was naturally a supporter and assumed from his past history that he would be too. At a neighborhood get-together, the referendum came up. When I said that I was voting for it, I remember being surprised when he said that he would not. For him, money was not an issue. His children had benefited from their educations, and he generally was a positive person. What he next said was instructive. He noted that he had done his share

89

by supporting past referenda and paying substantial property taxes over the years. Now he said it was someone else's turn since his family would not longer benefit from any tax increase.

What is important to consider from these real life examples is that they highlight the importance of conducting a comprehensive referendum campaign. From my experience, the days of counting on a majority of the community to vote for increased school funding just because the school board supports it or because it is the right thing to do are gone. Today, referendum success is largely linked to winning over more than the traditional "yes" voters.

CONDUCTING A SUCCESSFUL REFERENDUM CAMPAIGN

A referendum is really more of a political than an educational process for which administrators are often unprepared and/or ill-equipped. Many will need the assistance of attorneys and financial consultants to guide them through the referendum process because they maybe unfamiliar with all the legal requirements including adopting a referendum question. Some referendum committees even hire consultants to assist them in the political process. What is probably most useful for you to understand is how to conduct a comprehensive referendum campaign, which will be discussed in this section. However, before we do let's distinguish between the two most common types of referendums: building bonds and operating rate.

Building Bond Referendum

A building bond referendum is primarily facilities-focused. Schools boards, who want to renovate schools, build additions, or construct new schools, can ask the local taxpayers for a temporary tax increase to generate a specific dollar amount to use for specified improvements. A building referendum is the preferred option when a school district lacks sufficient operating revenue or reserves to fund a major project. For example, if a school board wants to build a new elementary school but needs an additional $20M, the school board would ask the taxpayers for the authority to sell bonds through a referendum. If more than fifty percent of the voters approve, the school board is allowed to tax property owners for the $20M.

Once a referendum is approved by the voters, the school board can sell building bonds to pay for the project. Usually building bonds are paid back over a period of at least 15 years. Bond holders receive repayment of their principal with interest over some specified period of time from annual property tax proceeds.

One additional point is worth noting. Building referenda, which are "brick and motor" projects, generally succeed at a higher rate than requests for operating fund tax increases. From 1990 to 2010, on the average 58% of Illinois school building referenda have succeeded (IASB, 2010). During the April 2011 election, this figure was only 42%, which was still higher than the success rate for operating fund referenda (IASA, 2011).

Operating Referendum

The second type of referendum is designed to increase property taxes permanently for school district operations. Unlike a building referendum with a specified focus, school districts have greater latitude to choose how to use additional tax revenues generated through an operating fund referendum. Most often, these new revenues support educational programs and services. However, before discussing this type of referendum, an important consideration is to recognize the differences in referendum requests between tax-capped and non-tax capped school districts.

TAX-CAPPED (PTELL) SCHOOL DISTRICTS

According to the Illinois Department of Revenue, PTELL school districts are allowed to seek voter approval to increase property taxes. However, because of recent changes in the law, formulating a referendum question in tax capped counties has become more complex. Sections 18-120 and 18-125 of the Property Tax Code identify four types of referendum questions (Illinois Department of Revenue, 2011). Since these can be confusing, school districts will often employ financial consultants in order to select the most advantageous option.

NON-TAX CAPPED SCHOOL DISTRICTS

In non-tax capped school districts, the referendum process has remained essentially the same as in the recent past. When a school board seeks a property tax increase through a referendum, the district asks taxpayers to approve an increase in the tax rate of a specific fund.

The school board may levy the requested rate against the total taxable district EAV as long as the requested tax rate increase does not exceed the state maximum for a particular fund.

To illustrate this, let's consider an example. Here are our assumptions.

- The school district is asking to increase its tax rate for the Education Fund by fifty cents from the current $1.00 to $1.50.
- The overall district EAV is $100M.
- The district plans to levy the full fifty cent increase the first year.

Although the example simplifies the factors and does not include some provisions that school district leaders would normally consider if they were conducting an actual referendum, it does demonstrate the basic process.

To calculate the approximate effect of tax increase on increased school district revenues in the Education Fund, you simply apply the property tax calculation discussed in Chapter 2:

- EAV/100 X Tax Rate Increase = Additional Property Taxes
- 1,000,000 ($100M/100) X 0.50 = $500,000

If you are considering a property tax increase through a referendum, remember that you will want to seek professional expertise from an attorney or financial consultant to ensure that you meet all legal requirements.

PASSING A REFERENDUM

Given the complexity of passing a referendum, school boards and administrators must develop a comprehensive referendum campaign plan built around a network of multiple stakeholders. Complicating any referendum, though, are state laws, which disallow the use of school district dollars to fund the referendum campaign as well as restrictions on when and how school board members and district employees may promote the referendum (Braun, 2010). Consequently, "selling" the referendum falls to a large extent on local residents who must not only lead the process but work many hours. Clearly, school leaders must educate the community about the district's financial needs if they are to mobilize community support.

A solid referendum campaign has its roots at the school board, staff, and community levels. When the school district administration determines that the additional tax revenues are essential in maintaining current programs and services, educating the school board, employees, and local residents as soon as possible is a priority. A lack of understanding about why additional tax revenues are needed usually translates into a lackluster referendum campaign and, subsequently, a failed effort.

One key to success is school board support. Often, some voters look to board members for guidance. District administrators must convince school board members that a referendum is imperative. Without the support of all seven school board members, winning a referendum becomes even more difficult.

Since referendum success rests to a large degree on the comprehensiveness of the referendum process, a key question to consider is – What are the stages in a successful referendum campaign?

To illustrate how a school district might design a successful referendum campaign, let's consider one employed by a suburban Chicago school district which passed an operating fund increase after failing a prior referendum (Kersten & Armour, 2004).

Phase 1. Building Support

Whether you have failed a previous referendum or are initiating your first in several years, a critical step is getting your message out early through school-community education. Although school district administrators may use a variety of strategies to accomplish this, all include identifying key local leaders and invested stakeholder groups. A successful approach used by our sample school district administrators and school board members was to conduct a series of reflection meetings for community leaders, parents, and district employees several months before the actual referendum day.

These sessions served a variety of purposes including:

- Assessing why the prior referendum failed;
- Identifying potential referendum supporters; and,
- Identifying referendum leadership team members who could direct the campaign.

From these sessions, a core group of motivated, knowledgeable leaders emerged who formed the heart of the community-based referendum team.

Phase 2: Pre-Referendum Campaign

After building an initial support base, the referendum process entered the pre-referendum campaign phase. At this point, since the school board had not yet officially initiated a referendum, district administrators had the latitude to educate as many residents and staff members as possible about the school district's financial needs. It was during this critical phase that much of the referendum groundwork was laid including the development of a comprehensive referendum campaign plan. It is important to remember that once a school board votes to place a referendum on the ballot, legal restrictions limit school board and employee involvement. However, it is also important to remember that school board members do not lose their rights as citizens and can serve in an individual capacity on the referendum committee.

During this stage, a critical step was selecting a referendum leadership team, which was responsible for developing the actual referendum campaign plan. Since this was pre-referendum, the superintendent and other district administrators were actively involved in the planning process.

As is typical of most successful referenda, the leadership team organized the campaign around a committee structure. Although the number, type, and scope of committees may vary from school district to school district, I have identified below those employed by the case study district.

Voter Registration. As noted earlier, a key to a successful referendum campaign requires getting out the "yes" vote. A good first step is taking every opportunity to ensure that the supporters are registered to vote. Strategies included:

- Initially contacting the county for a list of registered voters;
- Mounting a voter registration campaign;
- Sending information to unregistered voters about registration procedures and district needs;
- Distributing information on absentee voting;
- Targeting certain age groups such as those 18 to 25 years of age who might not otherwise vote;
- Consciously establishing voter registration stations wherever and whenever possible. Through the county, volunteers can be trained as official registrars and school and community events can be turn into voter registration opportunities; and,
- Confirming voter registrations with the county just prior to the voter registration deadline.

The referendum leadership team used these voter registration activities to increase the likelihood of reaching the "yes" voters.

Public Relations. The leadership team also recognized the value of tapping into local community residents with public relations experience to serve on the public relations committee which was charged with:

- Creating multiple publicity pieces ranging from informational letters to brochures to yard signs; even producing a video;
- Selecting a campaign theme with which residents identified;
- Preparing logos, response literature, buttons, and other forms of communication targeted to specific age and special interest groups; and,
- Serving as a resource to other referendum committees.

The public relations committee was invaluable in getting the referendum message out to voters.

Outreach. School districts are becoming increasingly diverse. As a result, successful referendum campaigns target district diversity whether related to specific age groups or special populations. This district's outreach committee planned specific activities to reach these unique groups. In addition, another major responsibility of the outreach committee was canvassing voters, which will be discussed later.

Data and Technology. Today more than ever, technology can be utilized to generate information and create access to the general public. An important committee to include in the referendum planning process is data and technology. Any referendum effort requires gathering large amounts of data about the district and potential voters. Our sample school district's data and technology committee increased the efficiency of the campaign by:

- Synthesizing and analyzing election and voter data;
- Gathering and analyzing voter information; and,
- Providing technical assistance to other committees.

Fundraising. As noted earlier, state law prohibits school districts from using district funds to finance a referendum campaign. This raises the question – who will pay for such items as informational materials, advertising, supplies, and phone calls? The answer is the referendum committee. As a result, in our sample district, a fundraising committee composed of volunteers with fundraising interest and, in some instances, experience raised adequate dollars to fund all planned activities. It is important to remember that Illinois political disclosure requirements apply to the referendum committee.

Phase 3: The Actual Campaign

After the Board of Education officially authorized the referendum, the actual campaign began. At this point, the referendum plan was in place. The school district administration had explained the financial position of the district. Community members were well aware that a referendum was imminent. The stage was now set for the actual formal campaign to begin.

It is important to note that a school board should not initiate a referendum sooner than three months before election day. If you begin a formal referendum campaign too early, you might have difficulty maintaining a high level of positive momentum while also increasing the risk of organized opposition.

However, once the referendum is certified, much needs to be accomplished. Some good advice I once received from an experienced superintendent who passed many referendums can be summed up in three simple statements:

- Identify the "yes" voters;
- Forget the "no" voters; and,
- Win over the "maybe" voters.

This is how every campaign from the presidency to a school referendum is won.

Given these three focuses, the case study district Outreach Committee employed a sophisticated voter canvassing process. As the superintendent told me later, this was probably the most critical part of the political process because here was where they actually identified, primarily through personal contact, the perceived yes, no, and maybe voters. The canvass activities of the oversight committee included:

- Contacting as many eligible voters as possible to determine their voting inclination;
- Conducting a door-to-door canvass of registered voters who were thought to be supporters but had not been reached by phone;
- Personalizing the message by encouraging supporters to contact neighbors and friends; and,
- Reminding voters about the referendum through cards and letters from respected community members just before election day.

Phase 4: Election Day

After months of hard work, referendum day finally arrived, but the work of the committee was not yet complete. On this day, when anticipation and excitement built, it was important to remember that the focus of the referendum campaign was to get out the "yes" vote. Consequently, every effort was made to use these last few hours to meet this goal. Several strategic ways the referendum committee used their volunteers on election day included:

- Designating poll watchers who not only recorded those who voted but also identified potential "yes" voters who had not yet voted so they could be contacted. Poll watchers also monitored the fairness of the election, challenged negative comments made to voters from election judges, observed vote counting, and reported election results to the referendum committee after votes were tallied;
- Placing volunteers outside polling places to distribute literature and encourage a positive vote;
- Designating phone personnel to receive calls from poll watchers and assist with communication among other committee members;
- Using "runners" who walked the precincts reminding supporters to vote and later in the day contacting "yes" voters who had not yet voted;
- Manning election central to coordinate the day's efforts; and,
- Establishing a meeting spot for all election volunteers to gather to tally unofficial election results and later that evening host a victory party, which they did!

Nothing is more satisfying to school district stakeholders than the feelings associated with a referendum victory. All the planning and hard work has paid off. The school district will now be financially sound for years to come. Everyone can turn their attention back to their real priority – providing an outstanding education for district children.

However, for other school districts, continued referendum failures may ultimately lead to financial insolvency. This raises an important question – What happens when a school district's financial position deteriorates to the point that it is on the verge of insolvency?

SCHOOL DISTRICT INSOLVENCY

Although most school districts use a combination of revenue enhancements and expenditure controls to maintain financial viability, a few cannot escape financial crisis. These school districts usually have explored multiple options to increase revenues and failed several operating fund referendums. They have also "cut" educational programs and services to the point where only the most basic education is offered. In addition, they have exhausted almost all their reserves. When school districts arrive at this point and are on the brink of insolvency, outside intervention becomes a reality.

During the 1990s when a few school districts began to reach the insolvency stage, the Illinois State Board of Education (ISBE) in cooperation with the Illinois Legislature passed legislation entitled School District Financial Assistance which was designed to help school districts resolve their financial crises (105ILCS 5/1B-1 to 1B-22). As of FY12, eight school districts are designated by ISBE as "in financial difficulty," that is, nearing insolvency: Cahokia Community Unit School District 3, Cairo Unit School District 1, Hazel Crest School District 152-5, Harrisburg Community Unit School District 3, Lemont-Bromberek Community School District 113A, Proviso High School District 209, Round Lake Area School District 116, and Venice Community School District 3, (Illinois State Board of Education, 2012d).

FINANCIAL OVERSIGHT PROCESS

When school districts such as those above are near the point of insolvency, their school boards may ask ISBE to certify them in Financial Distress (105ILCS 5/1A-8). When school boards make this request, they are aware that they are relinquishing a significant portion of their decision-making authority for expenditures. They also become subject in mandated ISBE intervention.

Financial Difficulty

The first level of state intervention is Financial Insolvency. ISBE requires these districts to develop, adopt, and submit a financial plan within 45 days of certification. They also are required to report regularly to the State Board of Education and provide reports documenting such items as budget data, financial statements, and other information as requested as requested by ISBE. (Braun, 2010). At the present time, Cahokia Community Unit School District 3, Harrisburg Community Unit School District 3, and Lemont-Bromberek Community School District 113A are at this level. If these school districts are unable to achieve solvency, they will most likely move to the next oversight level, Financial Oversight Panel.

Financial Oversight Panel

The second level of state intervention is the financial Oversight Panel process. The school district voluntarily requests that ISBE designate a Financial Oversight Panel (FOP) composed of three board members appointed by the state superintendent of schools. The FOP's primary purpose is to exercise financial control of the district by taking such actions as approving expenditures and the annual budget. The goal of the FOP is to help the district return to solvency (Illinois State Board of Education, 2012 d). If, however, the FOP determines that additional oversight is necessary, the panel may petition the ISBE to establish a School Finance Authority (SFA).

School Finance Authority

The SFA is a five member board appointed by the state superintendent of schools to replace the FOP. Its members must include two school district residents and three non-residents usually with school finance backgrounds who serve two to three years terms. What is unique about the SFA is that ISBE in cooperation with the state legislature writes school district-specific legislation establishing the SFA that must be approved by the legislature and signed by the governor. The initial term of the SFA extends from three to a maximum of 10 years (Illinois State Board of Education, 2012d).

In addition to the responsibilities of the FOP, the School Finance Authority has even greater control over the school district's financial management including actions such as:

- Approving the annual property tax levy;
- Issuing certain types of debt;
- Making expenditure reductions; and,
- Bargaining employment contracts.

One other important difference is that the School Finance Authority employs a management team that includes a chief executive officer (CEO), chief financial officer (CFO), and a chief educational officer (CEDO). It is not uncommon for the CFO and CEDO to be current district administrators while the CEO usually is employed from the outside. This team manages the district and reports to the SFA rather than the elected school board. However, the CEDO, similar to traditional superintendent, focuses on the educational aspects of the district and also works directly with the school board.

The SFA may choose a different management model as deemed necessary. For example, the SFA may decide to maintain the current administrative staff and not employ a separate CEO. In any event, once the SFA is in place, a two board governance structure emerges.

As you might imagine, the shifting of authority for all financial decisions to the SFA can create some management and political issues especially if the school board and SFA do not work collaboratively together. However, because of the need to address tough financial decisions, the SFA was purposely designed to operate independent of the school board and voting public (Kersten, 2006).

Dissolving the Financial Oversight

Since this legislation was initially approved, ten school districts have functioned under one of the levels of ISBE oversight. Some school districts were ultimately dissolved or annexed to neighboring school districts while oversight was dropped in another. In others, school districts emerged from oversight. In fact, one is presently designated by ISBE as the category of "Financial Recognition." These are the most likely results for school districts that emerge from oversight (Illinois State Board of Education, 2012d).

SUMMARY

In Chapter 9, we examined both how school districts use the referendum process to generate much needed school district revenues as well as the Illinois financial oversight process defined in law for those school districts who are near insolvency. These two scenarios illustrate the importance of financial planning along with the impact of wide variances in school funding throughout Illinois.

Chapter 10

Emerging Issues in Illinois School Finance

As I noted in the financial planning chapter, school administrators must accept the reality that as they plan for the future, they must be prepared for the unexpected. Because public education is so closely tied to the state legislative process and political realities, school administrators must pay close attention not only to what is happening at the state and national levels but also anticipate what issues might emerge in the near future. In this chapter, several important school finance issues which have or may have impact public education are discussed.

EQUITABLE FUNDING LEVELS

The wide variances in per pupil spending which impact both the scope and quality of educational programs and services in Illinois public schools is a real dilemma. The gap is large and may continue to grow. A CBS news reporter recently highlighted this dramatic inequity when she wrote a story about two Illinois school districts. She reported that Rondout School District in Lake Forest leads the state in per pupil spending at approximately $22,000 per child. Ranking at the bottom was Taft Elementary in Lockport which spends approximately $5,500 per student (McCall, 2007). Since the Illinois Constitution does not require equity, any solution to this problem lies with the legislative process. However, even at the legislative level, here are no easy answers to this dilemma since the underlying problem in Illinois is a lack of sufficient revenue.

The issues of equity and adequacy are not likely to disappear. Without a change in the Illinois Constitution or a dramatic infusion of new revenues, the vast discrepancies in funding and access to education opportunities will continue to be a state-wide issue.

SCHOOL FUNDING REFORM

Back in the early 1990s, a major finance topic which regularly dominated the school finance reform discussion was imposing a tax cap on property. As an assistant superintendent at the time, I, similar to many of my administrative colleagues, worried each time the state legislature met because we feared that something onerous would emerge from the legislative session. However, we knew that year in and year out, various governors had appointed finance commissions whose work ultimately resulted in no change or at best some tinkering with funding formulas. We learned that as any sweeping changes were unlikely to occur.

This was the prevalent feeling among many of my administrative colleagues as the issue of tax caps surfaced once again. We assumed that by the end of the legislative session clearer heads would ultimately prevail and that legislators would never be able to summon the votes necessary to pass tax cap legislation. In the recent past, there had been ongoing rhetoric about tax caps but no actual action. We believed that our local political leaders would ultimately recognize the negative impact tax caps would have on the financial viability of property tax dependent school districts. However, to our surprise, we suddenly found ourselves with tax cap as a result of a political compromise. This action changed forever how many of us view the legislative process.

In recent years other school finance reform initiatives have occupied the political agenda. One, which continues to receive substantial attention, is the property tax swap. Under this scenario, Illinois property taxes would be reduced and replaced with an increas in the level of state income taxes. On the surface, this makes a great deal of sense to the general public who as we have seen are generally anti-property taxes. To the average person it makes more sense to fund schools through increased income tax rates since those with higher incomes would shoulder a much greater burden for school funding.

Proponents argue that a state income tax approach would generate more revenue for schools which could be distributed to school districts more equitably thereby reducing the wide variances among school districts dollars spent per student. They point out that basing the funding system on income versus property taxes would help ensure equitable educational programs and services since the revenues district receive would not be as dependent on local property wealth.

Opponents counter that once school funding shifts from the property tax which is essential free of the state political process and a highly reliable source of school district revenue to an income tax based system, education funding will be reduced in property wealthy districts because the revenues lost will not be replaced dollar for dollar under the new funding model. Rather the stability of the property tax as a source of revenue would be replaced by an annual state budgeting process which would place a greater percentage of school revenues into political-based legislative process. Opponents caution that many school districts would actually experience a reduction in school district revenues.

As school funding reform initiatives such as the tax swap are proposed and debated, local school administrators, school board members, and other stakeholders would be wise to ensure that they are informed on the issues and prepared to articulate their positions through the political process.

TAX CAP AND INFLATION

Do you remember the late '70s to mid-'80s when many educators were expecting raises in the six to ten percent range? How soon we forget! For many years now, we have lived in an era marked by low rates of inflation. As discussed in Chapter 5, the annual rate of inflation has remained below the maximum tax cap level of 5%. However, in the future, maybe even the not too distant future; we may experience annual inflation rates exceeding five percent. Think for a moment what the impact would be on school budget deficits if inflation reaches seven percent or more and property tax extensions are capped at five percent. School leaders must be aware of the potential impact increases in inflation will have under PTELL.

BUSINESS PROPERTY TAX APPEALS

In the district where I was superintendent, it was common for large business property owners to regularly appeal their property tax assessments. In many instances, individual school district found themselves at a severe disadvantaged when fighting these appeals to preserve their tax bases. As a result, school districts and other local governmental units throughout the suburban Chicago area recognized the mutual benefits of banning together to collaborate in their fight reduce the effects of appeals filed within the property tax appeal board. Business leaders quickly learned that they could either use the legal process available to them to win a property assessment reduction or negotiate a compromise settlement with the taxing bodies.

In our school district, we regularly experienced business property tax reductions of as much a $1,000,000, some of which was for past years since the time required processing the appeals generally extended out several years. Since our school district was tax capped and tax rates usually below the maximums, we could recoup the loss of these business property taxes in future years by increasing the property taxes of other taxpayers. However, we experienced real property tax revenue loses for prior years because these dollars were rebated without an option to recover them.

School administrators and subsequently school boards need to be vigilant in not only fighting business property tax appeals but also staying informed on ongoing changes in the legal process. In fact, local governmental consortiums need to monitor all as aspects of the business tax appeal process, lobby legislators to increase school district standing in the appeals process, and even propose new legislative remedies. Since businesses will continue to seek new and even creative approaches to reduce their property taxes, this issue will remain an ongoing concern in the future.

FUNDING SHORTFALLS

A continuing issue in Illinois school funding, especially during a weak economy, is state cash flow and delays in property tax bills. In recent years, the state has had to postpone some revenue disbursements to school districts due to either a lack of adequate state revenues or the inability of the legislature and governor to pass a state budget in a timely fashion. Inefficiencies in the tax assessment process have also caused significant delays in sending our property tax bills. For some school districts, particularly those with limited reserves, this has resulted in the short-term borrowing or at least a loss of interest revenue on reserves. With the ever increasing demands for state funding across numerous areas and a weakened economy, this issue will likely continue to impact local school districts.

PENSION UNDER-FUNDING

A growing concern throughout the state is the under-funding of the Teacher Retirement System. For decades, the state has failed to fully fund its required pension obligation thereby weakening TRS's long-term financial stability. Although the contribution rates of pension system participants and more recently school boards have increased, these alone are not sufficient to fully fund pension liabilities. Because of the lack of full state TRS funding and increasing pension obligations related to retiree longevity, a more permanent solution to the under-funding problem must be found.

During recent years, the Illinois Legislature has changed pension benefits for new public school employees. More recently, the legislature is actively considering additional ways to reduce pension benefits for current and even retired employees. However, because of Illinois Constitution provisions, they are limited in what they can do.

Under recent discussion are several proposed changes. First, the legislature is discussing shifting future state pension obligations to school boards. At the same time, they are proposing that teachers who want to maintain their 3% compounded COLA will have their salaries frozen at their FY 13 level for future pension contributions. They would also lose access to TRS health insurance. Those, who want to avoid these restrictions, would have to agree to a non-compounded COLA increase of one-half of CPI but no more than 3%. Although no agreement was reached during the spring 2012 legislative session, these are popular political topics that are likely to remain part of the state legislative agenda for the foreseeable future.

PACE OF LEGISLATIVE ACTION

Illinois has a long tradition of broad-based involvement in legislative decision-making. Historically, the two political parties have taken different positions on many legislative issues. This tended to stir considerable public debate on major legislative initiatives. As part of this process, the public, especially those most affected by the legislation, were brought into the debate.

How quickly times have changed! Recently, the Illinois legislature has passed significant legislation such as pension reform in record time without substantial public comment. Often the differences in positions between the two political parties seem less clear. This change reflects a national mood. It is more popular than ever to be anti-tax and anti-union.

As a result of this shift, school boards, administrators, and employee groups should expect to have less influence on issues that affect them directly. They must monitor state and federal legislative action closely and be prepared to voice their opinions quickly and forcefully. Today, almost any legislation can pass in Springfield in record time.

SUMMARY

In this chapter, we have examined several imminent issues in Illinois school finance. This list is far from complete. What is important to remember is that school leaders must not only focus on the day-to-day operations of their school districts, but also maintain a keen awareness of both immediate and potential school finance issues.

Closing Thoughts

In this book, I have discussed the major topics in Illinois school finance that impact both sides of the school finance equation: revenues and expenditures. Hopefully, I have met the 7-Eleven test by making school finance more understandable for a wide audience of interested stakeholders, including those who are employed or have a vested interest in public education. In order to provide our children with a world class education that will allow them to lead productive and self-satisfying lives, we must all share responsibility for fully funding our system of public education. An important first step is to understand the basics of school funding in Illinois.

References

Alexander, K., & Alexander, M. D. (2005). American public school law (6th ed.). Belmont, CA: Thompson Learning, Inc.

Benson, C. M. (2006). Tax increment financing. Journal of School Business Management. 18(2), 11-17.

Beyer, B. M., & Johnson, E. S. (2005). Special programs & services in schools: Creating options, meeting needs. Lancaster, PA: Pro Active Publications.

Boer, H. (2004). Student activity funds need good policies. The Illinois School Board Journal.72 (2).4-5, 29.

Braun, B. A. (2010). Illinois school law survey (10th ed.). Springfield, IL: Illinois Association of School Boards.

Brimley, V, & Garfield, R. (2004). Financing education in a climate of change (8th ed.). Boston, MA: Allyn and Bacon.

Center for Tax and Budget Accountability. (2009). Illinois' school funding formula and general state aid. Chicago, IL: Author. Available from: http://www.ctbaonline.org/Education.htm

Chicago Public School. (2008). CPS department of human services. Chicago, IL: Author. Available from http://www.cps.k12.il.us/

Chicago Teacher Pension Fund. (2012). Member information. Retrieved July 27, 2010 from http://ctpf.org/general_info/publications.htm

Fritts, J. (2008). Essentials of Illinois school finance (4th ed.). Springfield, IL: Illinois Association of School Boards.

Guthrie, J. W. (Ed.). (2003). Encyclopedia of education (2nd ed.). New York, NY: Macmillan Reference USA.

Hennessy, E. (2007). Proposed financing schedule. Chicago, IL: William Blair and Company.

Hennessy, E. (2012). Bond Issues presentation, Chicago, IL: William Blair and Company.

Herman, E. & Kownacki, M. (2008). Cook County board approves Houlihan's proposal to reduce assessment levels. Available from http://www.cookcountyassessor.com/info/news/inthenews01.asp?ID=193

Houlihan, J. M. (2009). Cook county assessor. Retrieved July 6, 2009 from www.cookcounty assessor.com/1025.aspx

Illinois Association of School Administrators. (2012). Property tax cap map. Retrieved April 16, 2012 from http://www.iasaedu.org/index.php?option=com_content&view=article&id=178:yooslider&catid=58:the-project&Itemid=163

Illinois Association of School Administrators. (2011). Illinois school referendum results - April 5, 2011. Available from: http://www.iasa.org

Illinois Association of School Boards. (2006). Where does the lottery money go? {Brochure}. Springfield, IL: Author.

Illinois Department of Revenue. (2012). Illinois Revenue. Author. Available from http://www.revenue.state.il.us

Illinois Municipal Retirement Fund. (2012). Your Benefits Under IMRF. Author. Available from: http://www.imrf.org

Illinois ranks second in reliance on local revenue. (2007, July). Illinois School Board News Bulletin, 7, 10.

Illinois State Board of Education (2012a). 2011 annual report. Available from: http://www.isbe.net/reorts10/report.pdf

Illinois State Board of Education. (2012b). School Finance. Author. Available from http://www.isbe.state.isbe.net/finance/default.htm

Illinois State Board of Education. (2012c). General State Aid Formula - FY11 Overview. Author. Available from http://www.isbe.state.il.us/funding/pdf/gsa_overview.pdf

Illinois State Board of Education. (2012d). School business services. Author. Available from http://www.isbe.net/sbss/default.htm

Illinois Teacher Retirement System. (2012). Employer Bulletin: Tier II Annual Salary Rate and Credible Earning Limitation. Author. Available from http://trs.illinois.gov/subsections/employers/pubs/bulletins/12-04.pdf

Internal Revenue Service. (2012). Retirement plans frequently asked questions. Available from http://www/irs.gov/retirement.

Kaiser Family Foundation. (2012). Employer health benefits 2011 annual survey. Retrieved March 11, 2012 from http://chbs.kff.org

Kersten, T. A. (2006). State financial oversight: An option for insolvent school districts. Journal of School Business Management, 18(2), 8-12.

Kersten, T. A. (2008). Understanding new growth under the Illinois property tax extension limitation law (PTELL). Journal of School Business Management, 20(1), p. 15-21.

Kersten, T. A., & Armour, N. (2004). Education fund rate increase: You can pass it. Journal of School Business Management, 16(2), 36-43.

Kersten, T. A., & Dada, M. (2005). Skyrocketing healthcare costs: Is there a cure? The Journal of School Business Management, 17(1), 17-24.

Lincoln Investments. (2012). Limit for 2001-2012. Author. Retrieved April 12, 2012 https://www.lincolninvestment.com/res/lib/pdfs/HO213%20contribution%20limits_03-12.pdf

Local Governments' Guide to Tax. (2012). County School Occupational Tax. Author. Available from http://www.revenue.state.il.us/LocalGovernment/Overview/HowDisbursed/PTAX1002-8-C.pdf

McCall, K. (2007). Tale of 3 schools: Does funding lead to success? Chicago: IL: CBS Chicago. Available from http://cbschicago.com/specialreports/education.funding.tale.2.551121.html

Mesic, P. (2007). The power of the PTA. North Shore Magazine. 30(8), 34-36.

Our Lady of Angels Fire Memorial. (2008). Our Lady of Angels (OLA) school fire December 1, 1958. Author. Available from http://www.olafire.com/OtherFacts.asp

Retiree Fundamentals. (2008, Spring). Illinois Municipal Retirement Fund Newsletter, 23, 2.

Teachers' Retirement System. (2012). Springfield, IL: Author. Available from http://trs.illinois.gov

The Illinois Tax Increment Association. (2012). About TIF. Springfield, IL: Author. Available from http://www.illinois-tif.com

U. S. Department of Education. (2007). Special Education & Rehabilitation Services Archived: A Twenty-Five Year History of the IDEA. Author. Available from http://www.ed.gov/policy/speced/leg/idea/history.html

U. S. Department of the Treasury. (2012). Health Savings Accounts - 2011 Indexed Amounts. Retrieved April 16, 2012 from http://www.treasury.gov/resource-center/faqs/Taxes/Pages/HSA-2012-indexed-amounts.aspx

White, J. (2007). Illinois handbook of government 2007-2008. Springfield, IL: Illinois Secretary of State.

Yudof, M. G., Kirp, D. L., & Levin, B. (1992). Educational policy and the law (3rd ed.). St. Paul, MN: West Publishing Company.

Index